Eyes Up, Heels Down

by

Karen A. Stansbury

Lakeland Terrier Press, LLC

Lakeland Terrier Press, LLC
P.O. Box 181
Washington Depot, CT 06794

Cover cartoon by Dave May, Custom Cartoon Art
Cover design/layout by Deb Tremper, Six Penny Graphics
Logo design by Kelli Mincey, Cre8tive Mind Designs

Printed in the United States of America

Eyes Up, Heels Down is a work of fiction. Names, characters, places,
and incidents either are the product of the author's imagination,
or are used fictitiously. Any resemblance to actual persons,
living or dead, events or locales is entirely coincidental.

Contents

CHAPTER ONE
Psychic Vampires..3

CHAPTER TWO
Ginny..12

CHAPTER THREE
Angela..24

CHAPTER FOUR
Shamanism..35

CHAPTER FIVE
Vicky..51

CHAPTER 6
First Battle Won..64

CHAPTER SEVEN
CAPW..75

CHAPTER EIGHT
Randy..81

CHAPTER NINE
Telepathy..90

CHAPTER 10
Ginny's Story..102

CHAPTER ELEVEN
Lake Washington..114

CHAPTER 12
Rowing..124

CHAPTER 13
Erik..136

CHAPTER 14
Scissors *146*

CHAPTER 15
Mutants *150*

CHAPTER 16
Rowing Camp *157*

CHAPTER 17
Fraud *167*

CHAPTER 18
Suicide *172*

CHAPTER 19
Justice *181*

CHAPTER 20
Nantucket *188*

CHAPTER 21
Mencken *204*

CHAPTER 22
Deposition *212*

CHAPTER 23
Soul Retrieval *224*

CHAPTER 24
Trial *231*

CHAPTER 25
Freedom *246*

Recommended Reading *259*

About the Author *261*

Nothing can bring you peace but yourself. Nothing can bring you peace but the triumph of principles.

Ralph Waldo Emerson

CHAPTER ONE

Psychic Vampires

I was an undergraduate at Vanderbilt University during the Dark Ages. This was a time when a young woman only attended football games if she had an escort, and a corsage, and fraternity men only dated women who were members of the right sorority.

I was an alumna of Gamma Gamma Lambda Sorority. Known as the "Gotta Get Laid" Girls, we had a house on Kensington Place, and an excellent rapport with the fraternity across the street. On Friday afternoons the sisters would foregather on the lawn to watch the young men play lacrosse in their boxers.

Over twenty years later, this entertainment was even more appealing.

"They've stopped sewing their flies shut," Cathy commented, sitting down and handing me a hard lemonade.

"So I've noticed."

"And I think they may be waxing their legs now," noted Andrea.

"I'd forgotten what a near naked eighteen year old boy looks like," sighed Suzanna.

"Probably for the best."

Helene, our pledge class president, perched on the arm of my chair. "Who all's comin' from our year? Anyone know?"

"About thirty of us so far," Cathy replied, "which is a huge improvement over turn out for the fifteenth."

"My soon to be ex-husband has a theory about college reunions," I volunteered. "He says that the twentieth is when we can really start to relax and have fun. We're too busy with careers and raising children in the early years."

"We have more money now, too."

"Not me!" Mary exclaimed. "I've got two kids in college."

"That's cause you got knocked up durin' our senior year, doll baby," Helene said.

Suzanna struggled out of her chair. "Well, I'm heading for the lunch tent. I sure can't drink like I used to. Come to think of it, I can't do a whole lot the way I used to. Good thing I don't care."

"That *is* the beauty of old age," I agreed. "We can creak our way from one meal to the next, not giving a damn."

"That's right," Helene said. "Amazin' how lookin' good isn't quite as important when there are no guys to impress."

"No more competition," Andrea added.

"Notice how we aren't taking nasty little shots at each other the way we used to?" Mary asked.

"None of us is datin' anymore sweetie!" Helene laughed. "Woops! You tuck that bad boy back in there, sonny."

Suzanna picked up her Hermès bag. "Any one harboring fantasies about teaching those darling children over there about the birds and the bees?"

"Hell yeah," I grinned. "But why crush their fragile young psyches?"

After lunch we reviewed our options regarding campus events.

"There's a classical concert at the School of Music," Suzanna read from her program. "A performance of *Guys and Dolls* at the theater, and a lecture entitled *Was Jesus Married?* at the Divinity School."

"Pass!" Helene replied.

"How about the film on the shifting of the continents, which is being shown at the Engineering School?" I suggested.

"I want to hear the talk on vampires!" Mary decided. "It starts in fifteen minutes at the Sarratt Student Center auditorium."

"That's *psychic* vampires, you ninny," Helene retorted. "It's psychological stuff, not old episodes of *Buffy.*"

"I'm all for it," Cathy sighed. "Anything to keep me awake till cocktail hour."

Vanderbilt, like most old universities, had begun life in 1873 as a small cluster of buildings that had spread out as the decades passed. Currently ranked as one of the top twenty private universities in the United States, it entailed ten schools, including distinguished legal, medical and business centers. The campus was a beautiful landscape comprised of lawns, walkways, and trees, effectively masking the city of Nashville, which encroached from every direction.

We followed the crowd of chattering alums into the student center.

Our speaker, Elena Foyle, PhD was an assistant professor in the Psychology Department.

"We are all familiar with 'players,'" she began. "We've worked with them, dated them, even married them. These people are users. They take, and they don't give back. Players are manipulative, selfish, inconsiderate individuals. They delight in passive aggressive behavior. Who can give me an example?"

A student in the front raised her hand. "Changing plans at the last minute, without apologizing, and then acting as if it was the other person's fault, or problem."

"Excellent. In the social setting, they are the dates who leave us hanging, or use us to fulfill some undisclosed agenda, whether it is sex, money, or entrance into a specific group. In the business arena, these are the folks who alter passwords without notice. They tamper with websites, control money, send out email scams, and pit employees against each other. They collect opinions and ideas from others, and then rearrange them as their own, having contributed nothing of value themselves. Their goals are to take as much knowledge or experience as they can, create as much drama as possible, and then sit back to watch the show. Once they have gleaned what they can from the group, they move on. And finally, on a global level, they destroy our planet. They sap its resources, poison its air and water, and abuse its inhabitants.

"What is it like to be in a relationship with a passive aggressive person?"

A man in his thirties replied. "Horrible, because the other partner is never on solid ground."

Dr. Foyle nodded. "It is impossible to maintain a healthy, nurturing, supportive relationship, at any level, with such a person. These individuals implant themselves into your life as a friend, colleague, or lover. They use charm, and play the role for a time, usually until they feel that you are hooked, and then the draining begins. Women, who have been culturally trained to be the victims of other people's needs, are particularly vulnerable. These predators cannot be rescued, so don't waste time or emotional energy on them. They don't want help, friendship, or love. They want to dump their baggage on another person, and get an energy boost in return. If they are called on their selfishness, the reaction is one of breezy indifference to the individual who is the recipient of their behavior." She paused. "Now, who can tell me what the term 'psychic vampire' means?"

A low murmur arose from the audience, but there was no response.

"The original blood sucking myth emerged from the concept that these monsters were capable of sucking the life force from unsuspecting humans, and animals, thereby killing them. We in the mental health community tend to stick to more academic terms: borderline personality disorder, narcissistic personality disorder, sociopath, passive aggressive behavioral tendencies. However, I am also trained in Shamanism, and energy healing. The terminology under that heading is more descriptive. Psychic vampires are humans who suck energy. They are also capable of what is known as psychic attacks. That is to say, such persons are capable of sending negative energy, in the form of abusive thoughts or 'thought bombs', to another person or group.

"If you are shaking your head in disbelief at this moment, ask yourself the following question: Have I ever felt drained, or emotionally depleted, just by being in the same room with another person? If the answer is yes, then I can guarantee you that this friend, colleague, neighbor or spouse is a psychic vampire. He or she is siphoning off your positive energy for his or her own use, and leaving you nothing in return."

A hand went up in the back of the auditorium. "I've definitely felt that way, many times, especially around my former boss. Is this energy transfer dangerous?"

"Potentially, I'm afraid so. Once your energy level is brought down, you leave your weakened body open to fatigue and physical disease, as well as mental and emotional disturbances such as depression, anxiety, and loss of sex drive. Psychic vampires are not necessarily evil; they are damaged individuals, operating from a fundamental emptiness, and they need a host victim to survive. The host may be a lover, a child, even the family dog.

Their slurps of energy are temporary, and the vampire requires regular attacks to keep his or her energy at the desired level. They get a high from the emotional reactions that are engendered by their behavior.

"Energy vampires tend to feed most from anger, and the feeling of power from controlling another person, or groups of persons. If permitted, they maintain an emotional roller coaster, whereby everyone around them is reacting to their behavior, but unable to pinpoint the source. Psychic vampires have an innate knack for pushing buttons and fanning fires. They exploit good people. They can be pathological liars who think nothing of betraying someone who loves them. They have no conscience; no sense of shame or guilt. The best way to defuse their behavior is to avoid reacting to them. Without a response, they have no power or control, and the attempted psychic suck is defused. They must look elsewhere to feed. Be wary. If an energy vampire knows that you've blown their cover, they can become vicious.

"How do you know when you've been a victim of a psychic attack, or energetic hate mail? Personally, I know because I feel like I've just taken a hard punch to the gut. I've also experienced nausea, headaches, and an inexplicable urge to run in the other direction. There is a heaviness in the air, like thick fog, and just as confusing. Reactions vary. I've had patients tell me that they feel overwhelming fear, or loneliness. Others have nightmares, or can't sleep at all. Whatever your particular symptoms, I'm going to share with you some sure fire protections. Psychic vampires refuse to take responsibility for their own actions. It is imperative, there-fore, that you do.

"First and foremost, stay healthy, in both the physical and emo-tional sense. The stronger you are, the less likely you will react to a psychic vampire. Second, stay in tune with nature, and with animals, especially your pets. The more grounded you are, the more protected.

"Third, laugh. You'd be amazed how much negative energy can be pushed away by good humor. Fourth, never, ever give up your power to anyone. You are the final say on your life.

"And finally, use simple, yet powerful visualizations to repel bad energy. Some examples are building walls, or armor around yourself, or surrounding your body with a white bubble or golden net. Some people burn sage, bang drums, or ring bells, to break up bad energy. My own invention is gigantic industrial powered fans circled around me. Face them out, and flick the switch. You have the image of blowing your attacker into the next room. It completely disarms them. I've actually giggled a few times using this one."

Mary raised her hand. "Can you tell us about Shamanism, and energy work?"

Dr. Foyle smiled. "I teach whole courses on those topics! For our purposes today, Shamanic healing is employing ancient practices in modern times. Just be open to the concept that everything is energy, good or bad, and that good energy keeps us healthy and powerful, while bad energy makes us sick and unhappy. Think of childhood trauma, or a failed marriage as bad energy. You have to move bad energy out, to make way for the good. I use various methods to help patients; I call it integrative psychotherapy, and it employs both eastern and western methods of healing emotional problems. In my opinion, talk therapy alone is no where near as effective as energy healing, and I have the results to back up my thesis. Drugs are just band-aids, and completely useless. Again, that's my opinion, for any of you who are lawyers in the room."

There was a laugh. Helene elbowed me, and I nudged her back. I had a great deal to process with regard to my marriage, and getting through the next few months with my divorce.

"Don't you want to come back to school, just to take classes from Elena Foyle?" Andrea asked later, at the cocktail party on Alumni Lawn. She looked around and sighed. "I was so happy here."

All of my classmates at our table assented, but I remained quiet. My college years were too much like all my other years, to want to repeat them. But perhaps now it would be different. I had since learned that happiness cannot exist on a shaky, cracked foundation. One must heal the wounds from the past, in order to move forward.

Mary and I were sharing a double room in Scales, our old freshman hall. Helene and Cathy were in the room on the other side of the suite.

"God, do you remember the girls who lived here our first year? That fat broad from Alabama who looked like Miss Piggy, and that bossy female from Kentucky, who had the Scottish last name, and wore her clan kilts to class. They were always fighting, and the RA would have to intervene." Cathy snickered. "And the two lesbians in the next room, who got off on making out in front of everyone, even our parents. What a suite!"

"It was the eighties, Cath." Mary replied. "Nobody ever said the word lesbian in the South. Remember when the KKK wanted to march on campus?"

"Remember when Theresa was gettin' married, and her parents pitched a hissy, because she was keepin' her maiden name? Whatever happened to her?" Helene asked.

"She's an engineer with NASA," Cathy replied. "I saw her at the fifteenth Reunion."

"What did you think of the lecture, Em?" Mary asked. "You've been so quiet all evening."

"I've decided that the second I get home, I'm going to Google search for shamans in my area," I grinned. "There's a great place to buy dried sage in South Norwalk. I've got a bad husband that I need to move out of my life. That visual of gigantic fans blowing him back to Dartmouth is really working for me!"

"HERE WE GO VANDY, HERE WE GO!" Helene hollered, waving her bourbon slush like a pompon.

Cathy began to chant my favorite sorority song: "Gamma Gamma Lambda girls are amaaaazing. With our friendliness and charm we'll drive you craaaaazy." We started the round, with my alto coming in last. How I had missed singing with my sisters. How I had missed my connection with them.

CHAPTER TWO

Ginny

Divorce can drive a rational person temporarily insane. Divorce litigation is an invasive and disgusting experience, whereby packs of strangers are suddenly nosing in one's personal affairs, controlling one's actions, and barking orders in one's face.

I'd been spouting this maxim to my clients for years, but I had never felt it on a visceral level until I was forced to experience it myself.

I had married a player. A controller. An abuser. A liar and a deceiver. And according to information recently received at my undergraduate alma mater, a psychic vampire.

The showdown had taken place just one month before. Nick had been served with a writ, summons, complaint, and notice of automatic orders, per Connecticut law. I had located a small house to rent near the beach, packed up my clothes and books, and moved there in November with my Lakeland Terrier, Abby. Ethan Allen in Norwalk had duly delivered all of my beautiful new furniture, bought with what credit was left on my Mastercard. Williams-Sonoma in Westport provided me with kitchen necessities, courtesy of what credit remained on my Visa. I was maxed out, but free.

My new home was a delightful little Cape Cod style house, with weathered shingles, gables, and white trim, located two blocks from the harbor in Southport, an affluent section of Fairfield, Connecticut. This area was reminiscent of Nantucket Island; elegance being its underlying quality. Southport was comprised of huge old homes, with glorious gardens and an unmistakable air of disassociation from the rest of town, which was reinforced by gated driveways and security signs. My tiny beach house sat on a half acre of land, and was outlined by hydrangea and lilac bushes, and large maples. The property felt safe and serene; the perfect escape for a woman who was preparing to live under siege.

It takes a long time to recover from abuse. In my marriage I had suffered from emotional, financial, and even sexual abuse. Looking back, it was astounding to me that I remained more than ten years in such an environment. At the time all I could focus on was survival.

Because I had taken this courageous first step to regain charge of my life, everything had changed. I had bypassed the usual go to counseling and get put on a pill route, and had begun work with a Reiki Master who was certified in Clinical Aromatherapy. Together we had cleared the bad energy from my past, enabling me to move forward. Each day was now my own, and with the exception of my dog and my horse, no one was dependant on me. Every pleasure was heart felt, every household chore, no matter how mundane, had a new energy, because I was doing it for myself. Best of all, I would never be forced to deal with Nick's kids for the holidays again.

While the divorce was pending, every dime I spent would be scrutinized. Printouts of my checking account activity would be reviewed, line by line. Credit card statements for the past three years would be analyzed. My Filofax date book was discoverable as evidence. Opposing counsel would be looking for any loophole that would place the cause of the breakdown of the marriage on my shoulders, Of course, my legal team would be entitled to play the same game. In the end, the only people who won in these cases were the lawyers. The process was an invasion of privacy closely akin to rape, and the Bar Association did nothing to regulate it.

The first battle in the War of *Carbury v. Bennington* was scheduled for November twenty-third, in Ludlow Superior Court. My friend and law partner Denise Frederickson had filed a Motion for Temporary Alimony, a Motion for Counsel Fees, and a Motion for Order. Nick was refusing to acknowledge that I deserved financial maintenance while I built my new law practice. He was also refusing to reinstate me as beneficiary to his life insurance policy, or his will.

Another issue was conflict of interest among the judges in Ludlow. With one exception, every judge currently sitting in Ludlow had either worked with Nick while he was on the bench, or had practiced law with him.

Denise and I discovered this last disturbing fact when we arrived for the hearing.

The Presiding Family Judge in Ludlow at the time was Aimée Colger-Smyth. A diminutive, bird like woman, she minced her way through the courthouse hallways in frothy cocktail dresses, and spike heels. She had a reputation for continuing cases, and favoring men.

I had my first jolt of 'all was not well' when Judge Colger-Smyth referred to our matter as the *Bennington* case, and began chatting off the record with Nick's lawyer, while Denise was out of the courtroom. Nick, a tall man with gray eyes and receding dark hair, stood to the side, a self satisfied smirk on his face. I took several deep breaths, and wrapped myself in white light.

Then I stood up. "Attorney Emma Carbury, your honor, on *Carbury v. Bennington*. Attorney Frederickson is out in the hall. Perhaps we should suspend discussion on this case until she is present." Translation: why the hell are you having an *ex parte* discussion in open court with my husband's lawyer?

"You're the plaintiff, aren't you?" Judge Colger-Smyth chirped. "You should not be addressing the bench."

"With all due respect, your honor," I began, feeling nothing of the kind, "I have an appearance in the file."

"Attorneys may not file *pro se* appearances in their own divorces!" The judge squawked. "Sit down!"

At this point in the drama, Denise walked into the room, and looked at me with confusion. I could resonate with her dismay. The judge was exhibiting bias for Nick's side, and she had just dismissed me as a professional colleague with a non existent rule. These were not positive signs.

Nick's lawyer plodded over to Denise and handed her a document.

Michael McAfee, a graying dullard shaped like a square, was the Darien real estate attorney who was Nick's stooge for the occasion of our divorce. Like many of our legal brethren, Mike was in awe of Nick's reputation, and oblivious to his arrogance, and lack of character. Neither one of these men knew anything about the practice of family law in Connecticut.

"For the record," Mike snarled at Denise, "I have just handed the judge my Motion for Disqualification of the Plaintiff's Attorney. I suggest that the Court continue this matter to the next available date."

I looked over at Nick, who was sitting across the aisle from me. I was astonished to note that his attention was focused solely on the judge. Was he sending her some kind of energy bomb? Colger-Smyth's eyes darted back to him regularly as she addressed the two lawyers in front of the bench.

Her honor piped up. "I have informed counsel that many years ago, Judge Bennington and I practiced in the same office. I do not anticipate that this fact will affect my ability to be fair to either party in this dissolution action. Is there any objection to my hearing these motions?"

"No your honor," Denise replied, stunned.

"Very well. Three weeks, counselors."

"What is their argument for trying to get you off the case Denise?" I demanded over lunch.

Denise pointed to the paragraph in question with a French fry. "He's claiming that as I have had what he refers to as "social intercourse with both the plaintiff and the defendant during the marriage" it would be an unfair advantage to you for me to continue as your lawyer. It's nonsense, of course. You and I were law school classmates; I was never friends with Nick, so no conflict. He's trying to rattle your cage Em. He knows you need money, and he's going to make you beg for it, hoping for an easy, low-ball settlement."

"Those men are just two black holes of energy suck. This delay tactic is a waste of court time, not to mention money. Money that could be in my pocket." I pushed my tuna wrap away, no longer hungry. "Nick's probably counting on a violent reaction from me, as well. That's what I always did in the past." I took a few deep breaths, and visualized the bad energy moving out the top of my head, like exhaust. "Let's fool them. They're assuming that we'll go into the next hearing, loaded for bear on their motion, right? How would you feel if I hired another lawyer? We reclaim our motions, so they all come up on the calendar at the same time, and my new hired gun will be ready for argument, while their motion is rendered moot?"

Denise perked up. "And they won't know it until the day of the hearing? They'll be focused in the wrong direction. That's brilliant! Who are you thinking of?"

"A male lawyer will even the odds a bit with Judge Come Hither. I'll send Donald Hall an email as soon as we get back to the office." Denise sighed. "I didn't feel comfortable challenging the judge today. I knew that if I did, it would come back to haunt me down the road, and we still have too many litigation cases pending in Ludlow. I don't care if this is the twenty-first century. The practice of law is still a good ole boy's club."

"It certainly is in Ludlow," I agreed, wondering just how well Nick and Aimée Colger-Smyth had known each other in the past. "Judges are touchy creatures as it is, always worried about their decisions being overturned by the Appellate Court. Aimée is unintelligent, inefficient, and a political butterfly. That's a deadly combination."

I stopped at Southport Nails to get a much needed manicure and pedicure. Normally, I found such spa treatments relaxing; I sat while lovely, gentle Korean women worked on my hands and feet, and massaged my shoulders. To my dismay, my attendant this time was a large, burly looking male, who filed my nails so hard and fast that he sliced open two of my toes. Later, as I sat at the drying table, he appeared behind me for a complementary back rub. His hands were rough and calloused, and eventually I emerged from the experience feeling man handled, and even more stressed and frazzled than when I walked in.

My horse was the love of my life. Joy and I had been together since she was flown over from Ireland at the age of three. She was a big, beautiful, super talented bay, and the wisest person that I knew. Joy had taught me unconditional caring, and spending time with her was instant happiness. I kept her clean, healthy, and fit. She kept me grounded.

In the spring I had decided to move Joy to a private horse farm in Weston, owned by my friend Lisa and her husband Jack. We had all agreed to relocate our horses to Hunt Fields Equestrian in Redding for the winter, to take advantage of their indoor arena. It was a sacrifice to leave our much appreciated autonomy for another show barn, with at least three A-Circuit trainers vying for lesson time in the indoor for four months. Even more disturbing, we would be paying an additional five hundred dollars a month for board, and our horses would be getting less than half of their usual turn-out time. It was the price we had all agreed to pay to keep riding all winter, but the added expense worried me.

Lisa had rented an old barn on the estate, next to the indoor, for our three horses, as well as Betsy and Sally's horses, her other boarders. The remaining stall was used as a tack room. Space was tight. The stalls were smaller than those in Lisa's sparkling new stable, and the walls were un-insulated. Joy's water bucket had already frozen over twice since we'd arrived.

We had barely settled in when our trainer, Olivia Thompson, decided to move her business to Vermont. We were forced to work with the professionals at Hunt Fields. As Joy was a jumper, I had no option. Ginny Sherman was the only competent big jumper trainer in the barn.

I had come to accept that there was a cosmic order to every situation that we faced, and that we were meant to learn from our choices and our experiences. Looking back, the disaster triggered by my decision to work with Ginny was completely predictable. But that Fall I was overwhelmed by a new home, a new law practice, and a new barn, as well as being under fire in the divorce. I was in for the lesson of my life.

My understanding was that we were expected to be grateful for this level of torture. It helped us to evolve.

Right.

Ginny Sherman had just turned thirty. She was tall; taller than my five foot nine, with the classic Equitation figure: long legs, minimal torso. Otherwise, she could have been my younger sister, with her blue eyes, dark brown hair, olive features, and booming laugh. We even drove the same eight-cylinder Audi, although my car was bright red, and hers was navy blue. Ginny's riding career was on a plateau of sorts. She had shown horses in many Grand Prix, and had accumulated a long list of prizes in the fourth, fifth and sixth places. There she hovered. The grooms often spoke of her Olympic aspirations, but I never heard her do so. She seemed content to teach riders of all levels, find horses for them, and babysit her clients to various A rated horse shows.

Ginny was enthusiastic about Joy's talent, and Joy appeared to trust her, which was all I needed to know.

"She has Grand Prix scope!" Ginny exclaimed, watching a video of a former trainer riding Joy in a power and speed class at Old Salem Farm. She bent toward the screen. "But I don't like how he's handling her. Look at her tossing her head. He's on her mouth too much."

Good. She was at least saying what I wanted to hear. Let's see her in the saddle. How long would it take before she gave me the classic trainer speech?

I sat on the mounting block and watched Ginny trot Joy over some poles. Joy was nervous at first. Her eyes seemed fixed, and her lower lip quivered, a sure sign of anxiety. Then Ginny took her over a few small jumps, and Joy relaxed. Ginny had nice quiet hands, and a lovely balanced seat. Most important, she had a healthy respect for Joy's strength.

"This is a lot of mare!" Ginny reported, hopping off. "Are you sure that she's not too much horse for you?"

Aha. The speech. I'd heard it every time from every trainer with whom we'd worked, with the exception of Olivia. What they were really saying was "let me convince you that I can find a better horse for you, and sell yours, so that I get a commission each way." This young woman had never seen me ride, and after only ten minutes with us, had no concept of my relationship with Joy. But they were the experts.

I smiled. "Oh, I'm sure. Joy is family. She stays with me. Always."

Immediate grin. "I agree with you that she's a wonderful horse. And she has such a pretty face. I'd love to help you in the saddle." I felt a kick in my mid section, like extreme nervous knots. What was going on here?

We agreed that Ginny would work Joy two days a week, and I could take lessons or hack as I chose. Ginny was amenable to the fact that showing was not in my budget for now. "My goal is to help you get to the point where you don't need me any more," she said.

"What do you think?" Lisa asked quietly, an hour later in the tack room. "I have my daughter signed up with Ginny for the indoor shows. Do you think she's a good trainer?"

I hung up my bridle, and put my boots back in my trunk. "She's good enough. But she's young, and intense. I can't put my finger on it, but something is odd. When you talk to her, it's as though two different conversations are going on at the same time. I'm a little uncomfortable, and I don't know why."

But Lisa wasn't interested in feelings. It was all about her daughter's riding career. "Ginny comes from a very wealthy family in Westport. They are Sherman Pharmaceuticals, and her mother is a big noise in the hunter/jumper world. As long as Ginny can handle Sharon's horse, I'm happy. Wally is too big and strong to be such a bully. He needs a confident rider."

"Ginny's good enough," I repeated. "Lisa, did you sign a lease for us to be here? Are we stuck until the end of March?"

"No, it's month to month, but they'd like thirty days notice. Why?"

"I just like to know what our options are."

My watercolor class buzzed with my good news. "Congratulations, Emma!" Sheila beamed. "I hear that your painting was accepted for the Connecticut Watercolor Society show."

"It's very exciting," Pam, our teacher, agreed. "They are particular. If you are admitted to one more show, you will be invited to become a signature member." Pam already enjoyed this designation; her paintings were signed Pamela Schultz, CWS.

"I'll keep painting then," I said. "I've brought a couple of new seascapes with me. Southport beach has definite potential as an artistic reference."

"You need soothing subjects," Pam said, wisely. "I remember our daughter was the same way when she was getting divorced. She'd spend days at our island house in the Thimbles, just reading and thinking."

I thought of the Discovery Requests that we had just received from Nick's lawyer, and privately agreed. It would take me days to produce all the financial information they were demanding. They even wanted Joy's insurance policy.

I worked steadily for twenty minutes until Pam moved over to my table. "I love the fall colors in the sea grasses," she commented, pointing with the handle of my rigger brush. "And I like the variation along the shore line, and in the background trees. Just be careful that they aren't too rhythmic. Nature isn't like that." She grinned. "Unless a landscaper comes in with clippers. Think wild and untamed."

I sighed. "That used to be me!"

"It will be again, and better than ever." Pam said. "Your paintings are sensuous, and you are so passionate about your animals, and helping people. Some day you will find a man who loves that about you. Have faith."

In October Denise and I had opened our new law practice in an old building on the Saugatuck River in Westport. Close to the train station, I-95, and the Post Road, it was an ideal location with a specific benefit; my office windows looked out on the river. As we were moving in, I had enjoyed watching the Westport Rowing Club members travel up and down the Saugatuck, usually accompanied by coaches in motorized launches, but sometimes solo. I made note of the wide variety of shells: eights, fours, and pairs, each rower using one big oar, known as sweep; or quads and doubles, each crew member rowing with two oars, or sculling. My favorites were the singles. Much more relaxed without the pressure of staying in cadence with other people, these rowers seemed to be having the most fun. As it was now early December, the boats were gone, and the river was freezing over. Seagulls and other water birds sat huddled on the deserted docks.

Driving back from lunch the following week, I was stopped at a light directly across from the rowing club. I watched members in suits walk through the big front doors with their work-out bags, and other members, clad in Lycra, some with yoga mats, get into their cars. On an impulse, I made a quick right into the lot, and parked my Audi in the visitor section.

The young man at the front desk buzzed the Membership Director for me, and within minutes I was taken on the full tour.

"Do you row?" The woman asked, as we strolled through the club common room, with snack bar, and into the boathouse. Rowing shells were stacked on shelves along the walls, and in the center of the room, dozens of electronic rowing machines, or ergometers, were lined up facing a center screen. "The teams are in winter training now," she explained. "We pull the boats out of the water in early November. We have a very competitive juniors program, and our adults, or Masters, have won the nationals several times."

"I have always wanted to learn," I said. "I kayak and canoe, and I have a show jumper, so my balance is pretty good."

"I suggest that you get started with a trainer now, working on the erg, so that you will have the proper positioning down before coaching on the water begins in April." The Director replied. "We offer private, semi-private, and group rowing lessons for novices. Once you're certified on the water by a coach, you are welcome to sign out one of the club boats when you wish. This is included in the membership, although erg training and rowing lessons are extra."

We walked through the ladies' locker room, and then upstairs to the workout facility.

"Above us is the studio, where we offer classes in yoga, Pilates, spinning, and various other cardio and weights workouts. The restaurant is over here."

The room was decorated, like the rest of the building, in a nautical theme, with deep blue carpet and window treatments, dark green upholstery, white bead board, brass fixtures, and old rowing prints on the walls. The balcony overlooked the river. I was hooked.

Back downstairs in the Director's office, I handed over my check, and was given a key card and a parking sticker. "I'll have one of the trainers email you about availability. You have to erg, before you can row. I suggest that you invest in some Lycra shorts, if you haven't already done so."

Elated, I drove up Riverside Avenue to our office. You have to erg before you can row. My new mantra.

CHAPTER THREE

Angela

Nick had left a voice message on my BlackBerry. "Emma, notice just came in from the Audi dealership that your lease is about to expire. I have no intention of cosigning another car for you. Also, I am sending you a copy of the ExxonMobil card bill. I expect you to reimburse me for any gas that you buy on the joint card from now on. Let me know if you want to see Macduff."

In just a few succinct sentences my dear husband had hit me with two psychic zaps: first, by threatening to take away my car and my gas card, and thereby my freedom, and second, by reminding me that I had left my beloved Welsh Terrier behind in Warwick, under his care, and that it was one of the biggest wrenches of my life to do so.

Remembering Dr. Foyle's lecture, I did not respond.

Instead, I took several deep, slow breaths, and emailed my new lawyer, Donald Hall. He emailed back that I should attempt to get a new lease on my own, and failing that, he would file an additional motion. "There is no point in trying to reason with those two bozos," he replied. "It's a waste of your money, and my time. Besides, we want to keep my involvement in the case quiet until the hearing. Go talk to the dealership."

An hour later I was sitting with Dave Pressman in Fairfield, going over my options.

"Thank god you made sure that your name was on the last two leases, Emma." Dave announced, offering me a bottle of water. "Otherwise, I don't think I could pull this off."

"Yeah, that was one smart move that I made in this marriage."

Dave looked sympathetic. "Listen, all the guys here agree. You should never have to put up with a jerk like that. He always acted too busy and important to have to interact with the likes of us. You can do SO much better."

"Thanks Dave."

"Now, about your new car. Red again, I presume?"

"Yes, please, with sun roof, heated seats, the works. My life style is on an upswing."

"You go girl! I think I can even get you the fancy chrome wheels. And the new model goes even smoother than you one you have now. You're going to love it."

I made arrangements with my insurance agent for the new Audi when it came in, dropping my name from our joint policy, and setting me up on my own. I then did the same with my health insurance, buying totally new coverage. I called ExxonMobil, and arranged for my own credit. I then cut up the marital gas card, and put it in the mail for Nick. As we had no other joint accounts, this was the last of the financial ties to the marriage, except for the final banging of the gavel.

"What a difference from the old Emma," announced my sister Kate, who had come down to dinner at the rowing club on Thursday night. "Look at you. You're in your own home now, with your own brand new furniture. You've got your own practice, a new car coming in that will be in your name only, and this very nice place to meet people, and learn to row. Do they let you have guests?"

"They sure do!" I said, reaching into my wallet. "I've already gotten you a stack of passes."

"Best of all, you are no longer reacting to Nick with the gale force that you were so famous for, not so long ago. The volatility is completely gone. What an impact a year makes!"

"It feels good to clear out old garbage, I admit."

"Are you still getting the dreams?"

"Yes, when I'm not too tired to remember them. Last night I watched as an antebellum female slave was being buried, with a circle of flowers on her head. No coffin, mind you."

"Pretty obvious significance. No more boring dinner events with Dartmouth cronies, or Navy buddies, or hockey teammates. No more house parties with his friends up in New Hampshire. Does the man do everything in a big group?"

"Of course. Suck all the energy you can, never give any of it up. No more arranged tours to Europe, stuck on buses with blue haired retirees. No more miserable, exhausting Christmases with his appalling kids. No more back breaking yard work. I'll never have to fold his boxers, or buy his bloody bananas again."

"Speaking of appalling, want to hear the latest about our dear mother?"

"Not really Katherine. I've cut Audrey out. I can't afford her vicious negative energy in my life right now."

"OK, I get that. But this is funny. She's dating!"

"No!"

"Swear. A widower from church, reportedly loaded."

"He'd have to be. Audrey is high maintenance."

"She also knows how to charm her way in, or out of anything. They're flying to Paris next week."

"We've been working on my anger toward her in Reiki. Marilyn has me sitting in front of the mirror every morning, saying over and over, I forgive my mother and accept that she did the best that she could."

"That's rather a frightening thought. Oh well, at least she's having fun in her golden years. And this Greg is keeping her occupied, which distracts her from targeting me, for a change."

Annie, my office assistant, buzzed me the next morning. "Your nine o'clock is in reception."

"I'll come out."

Angela Caxton was a local newscaster with a bright future, and a real loser of a husband. We'd been friends since our days at Ridgefield High, when we were both in Mrs. Ferro's honors English Literature class our junior year. Angela had married one of her journalism professors, and moved back to Ridgefield. Dick had several Pulitzer nominations under his belt, but hadn't done much of anything in the last ten years. He was content to watch Angela's rising star and capitalize from it.

"Emma, you're wonderful to see me so quickly, especially when I know that you want to get away from litigation cases, and do mediation only."

"Tell me where you are with the divorce right now."

"We've met with the Special Masters. They basically said that I'd have to give him forty percent of my assets."

"Really. What did your lawyer say?"

"He recommended their proposal."

"Fine. I'll call him and have him send me the file."

Angela let out her breath. "Oh good. Kent's a nice guy. He just can't handle Dick's attorney."

"Don't worry any more. Now, you said that there's an outstanding motion for exclusive possession?"

"Dick filed it. He changed the locks on my house. And it is *my* house, Em. I inherited it from my parents, I pay the mortgage, but since I moved out, he's trying to use it as leverage in the divorce."

"So much for the Automatic Orders. Whose idea was it for you to move out?"

"Mine. But Kent said that it would be all right."

"Has anyone asked for a pretrial with a judge?"

"No."

"That's step one. Did you bring copies of the financial affidavits?"

"Yes. Dick has my personal assets listed on his plus column."

"When I have everything in front of me, we'll have a meeting. Meanwhile, I'll call Judge Tuchman's clerk at Dover Superior Court and see what kind of time she's got, in terms of pretrials."

"Thanks so much." Angela relaxed in her chair. "How are you doing? How's precious Joy?"

"She's been deliriously happy at her all-day salad bar at Lisa's barn. This new winter situation is giving me pause, however."

"What's going on?"

"First, it's more money for a less comfortable place, and less turn-out. It's also a longer drive for me from Southport. But it's the new trainer who's really making me nervous."

"She's not competent?"

"No, she is. It's…this is going to sound wacky Angela. I feel very strong emotions coming from her, but I can't isolate what they are. There's a darkness all around her, like wood smoke, and I'm exhausted from spending just an hour with her. But it's not anything that she's saying or doing. She's an excellent, natural teacher, and she's terrific with Joy."

"Maybe it's something she's going through. Is she married? A boyfriend maybe?"

I winced. "Uh, if she's involved with a man, I'd be very surprised. She's hit on me several times."

Angela laughed. "She won't get anywhere there! I know you too well."

"This isn't funny, Ange. It's all done subtly, and it's really disturbing. I feel like I have no choice but to deal with this woman, at least until we go back to Lisa's in the spring. There's still the problem of finding another trainer once we do. I have to admit, there are times when I wish I had never started riding."

"Because of the money?"

"Partly. Nick is using Joy as a strategy in the divorce. But I could handle that nonsense, if I had someone I could rely on to help me with her. Someone without serious emotional issues. Professional horse people are a curious lot."

"So, Shakespeare's line should have read: 'The first thing we do, let's kill all the *horse trainers*?'"

"Absolutely. Lawyers are rank amateurs in their presence. Baby sharks in the tank of life."

"I just picked up a book that made me think of you. It's an analysis of the relationship between FDR and Winston Churchill. The author's done a good job. He's written from the humanist approach, rather than from the political."

"I'll suggest it to my Book Club."

Angela looked wistful. "You have a book club? How many are you?"

"You remember my friends Denise and Eliot from law school. Dottie is a paralegal in Nick's firm. Jane is the English teacher who is married to Nick's friend Pete. That's it, Why don't you come to our next meeting?"

"I'd love to. Put me on the group email." She began fussing with her wedding ring, sliding it back and forth on her finger.

"I'm going through this too, Angela. I know what it's like. Admitting defeat is difficult for women like us." I paused.

"Especially when you feel duped by someone in your own profession, and you used to look up to him."

"That's it in a nutshell, Em. I feel stupid, and deflated at the same time."

"It's going to get better, I promise. Meanwhile, what's the name of your book?"

I finally managed to make a stop at New Moon in South Norwalk. I admitted to feeling a combination of anxiety and embarrassment as I walked in to the store. There were racks of candles and oils, shelves of books and CDs on varying spiritual subjects, from living one's power, truth, and in the present, to angels, shamanism, dream analysis, sensual massage, and even fairies. In the center of the shop were numerous displays of spiritual paraphernalia: incense burners, bells, small gongs, drums, rattles, feathers, and bundles of herbs. In the back by the register was a glass case full of jewelry. A pungent citrus candle was burning, an electric fountain was cascading by the door, and overhead, Australian aboriginal didjeridu music was playing. It was certainly a multi cultural place.

The small blond woman at the counter appeared fairly mainstream. I explained that I had attended a lecture given by a shamanic healer, and that she had mentioned that burning sage would clear negative energy.

"I have smudges in mountain sage, and in sage/cedar combinations," she announced. "Do you have something safe to burn them in? If not, I recommend one of these stone dishes. You want to avoid sparks."

I decided on a couple of each of the smudge bundles, and also what resembled a white stone ash tray. "Do you mind if I browse?" I asked, taking out my wallet. "This is my first time in this store."

"So it all seems a little strange? I think it's ironic that ancient practices, whether North American, Asian, Australian, or European, have been labeled 'New Age.' It all boils down to the same thing."

"What is that, exactly?"

"Energy. Staying healthy and happy by bringing in the good energy, and clearing out the bad. Manifesting the life you want by visualizing it first. Respecting the earth. Thinking abundance and community, rather than scarcity and isolation. And living in the moment. The rest is window dressing."

I stopped and stared at the woman. She made it sound so simple.

"Do you own this store?" I asked.

"No, I'm just here occasionally, to help out a friend. She had an emergency, and luckily, I had some free time." She smiled. "I'm a massage therapist, and a shamanic practitioner. My name is Afton Oliver."

I made an appointment with Afton for my first shamanic session, at her home studio near the harbor. I also bought the aboriginal music CD. As I went to my car, a hawk swooped down from a tree, and hovered just above me. I could see its cruel beak and cold eyes, but for some reason, was not afraid. It made one loud call, and flew off.

My Book Club met at our office for the final discussion before the holiday season. Denise and I had decorated the conference room with spruce garlands and holly. Several bouquets of red and white roses mixed with amaryllis and greens were arranged on the book cases and in the reception area. We had a local caterer do a big party platter of appetizers, and the punch had a champagne kick to it. New files, and healthy retainers, had been coming in steadily, and we were both feeling grateful.

We were talking about Alice Koller's memoir, *An Unknown*

Woman, A Journey to Self-discovery. Angela, as our newest member, volunteered to do the plot summary.

"The action takes place in 1962. Alice has finally earned her doctorate in philosophy, but is stuck in a seemingly endless cycle of dead-end jobs, temporary housing, and relationships with numerous men that are doomed from the beginning. Feeling that her life has reached an intolerable level of misery, Alice rents a house in Siasconset, on Nantucket, and spends the winter there, hoping to sort out the source of her inability to be happy. Her only company is a German Shepherd puppy, bought for the occasion. Alice names him Logos. His other name however, is Sweet Puppy."

"Beautifully done, Angela," Jane replied. Jane, as the only English teacher in the group, led every discussion. "What would you all say is the major theme of this memoir?"

"The value of solitude?" Dottie suggested. "This young woman proves the importance of really getting away to reach the heart of one's personal problems."

"Mother-daughter issues are deep and painful?" Denise added. "And did anyone notice, she never does analyze her relationship with her dad, who is dying. Parents are always dually responsible."

"His illness is probably the trigger for her other feelings coming to the surface," I explained. "I know of what I speak. The same thing happened to me, but I ignored it, to my detriment."

"Don't you think that the solution was a bit prosaic, though?" Eliot replied. "Every high school kid learns in junior psych that childhood woundedness affects us all."

"Yes, but did they know that in 1962? I think this book was very advanced for its time," Angela said. "Not many women were achieving Koller's level of education. Most of us were born in the sixties, remember." She paused. "I think the message of this book is the definition of unconditional love. It's what every child deserves from a parent. It's what every person deserves from a relationship."

"But rarely gets," Denise remarked.

"And it's fifty years later. What does that tell you? Koller discovers that because her mother never loved her, she spent her life taking on roles that she didn't want to play, putting on a mask for the world, telling herself that she loved man after unavailable man, wanting to be rescued from it all. She ends up on an island in the Atlantic in the middle of winter, contemplating suicide. What does Koller decide in the end?"

"That we have to do what we want to do," I replied quickly. "And say what we mean. Nothing else matters. We must honor ourselves, first. Family, friends, lovers—they can't fill that void for us."

"What void?" Jane prompted.

"The one that tells us that our lives have no value. *Every* life has value. Every person has something to contribute."

There was a short silence. Then Denise: "Koller concludes that chastity has nothing to do with morality, which is someone else's imposed standard on women. Instead, she decides that chastity is a discipline that women impose upon themselves to ensure what she calls psychological purity. What is Koller saying?"

Dottie referred to her notes and opened her copy of the book. "She writes that chastity buys time. Time for a woman to really get to know a man, and then to trust him. Why can't every mother teach every child, male or female, this very important lesson?"

"Because they don't know it themselves," I replied grimly.

Eliot reached for another California roll. "I guess I was wrong," she admitted. "This book is still timely. Depressingly so."

I decided then to tell them about Ginny. "How should I handle this?" I asked, when I had finished. "I feel trapped because I really need her to help me with my horse. Yesterday she was putting a cooler on Joy when she suddenly covered my hand with hers. My stomach did a few loops into my throat, and a drumming sounded in my ears. Everything went white for a moment. I just don't understand it."

"What is all of this telling you, Em?" Angela asked, gently. "Do you think that you're attracted to her?"

"A week ago I would have said absolutely not. And then Sunday night I had a dream. It was Ginny, in bed, and one bare leg was curved outside the covers. She was smiling, well, almost leering."

"Were you in the dream, or just watching?" Denise wanted to know.

"Just watching."

"Then it could be anything, right? I'm no expert on this stuff, but I bet there are a variety of reasons for dreaming about this female. Maybe it has to do with your divorce."

"I agree," said Angela. "Don't jump to conclusions. And I'd get out of that barn as soon as you can. Even if it means no riding until the spring. You should not feel this uncomfortable."

Dottie picked up the book again. "Koller talks about her gut reaction to that jerk who doesn't hire her because she refuses his pass, remember? She admits that the mistake was hers, because she was aware of her own discomfort with the situation, and yet she ignored the obvious signs. Listen to your inner voice, Em. Tell Lisa to give these people thirty days notice, and get out."

When I unlocked my front door later that evening, Abby came bounding down the stairs to greet me, barking gleefully. I picked her up, and hugged her tightly. Too tightly, apparently, because she growled in my ear. "Sorry Sweet Puppy," I said. "Do I ever tell you how grateful I am to you for being my best friend?"

Abby and Joy. No person, no thing, was as important to me as they were.

CHAPTER FOUR

Shamanism

I arrived at the rowing club at seven a.m., clad in Lycra shorts, to meet with my new coach. Christine was a recent college graduate, and a competitive rower. She put me to work right away.

We went out to the boathouse and located two ergs at the back of the room. Several club members were already working out, and music was blaring.

The ergometer was comprised of a big flywheel in the front of a monorail, a sliding seat, a foot rest that locked the feet in position, a handle which simulated the oars, and a small electronic performance monitor, mounted above the wheel. Christine checked to make sure that the damper on the flywheel was set between three and four.

I watched as she demonstrated the various parts of the stroke: the catch, the drive, the finish, and the recovery, back to the catch. "It's all about momentum," she said. "Your oars, or oar, if you're rowing sweep, will be in the water, moving you along. Most of the power comes from your legs and your core, as you push yourself back on the drive. Shoulders relaxed, arms straight. Your arms transfer this power to the oars. You want forward motion at all times. Don't pause at the finish—that's right. Your movements should blend together, to make the stroke smooth and continuous. You want an immediate recovery back up toward the catch. Arms away first, past your knees. Then your legs."

I glanced at the monitor. "What are those numbers?"

"Your strokes per minute is in the right corner. For our purposes right now, I want you to stick to around twenty. Later on, we'll build you up to twenty-four and higher. On the left is time rowing. Below that is your split, or your pace throughout your workout. For now, let's keep your split at 2:30. The little graph below is your force curve, which is the power of your drive. Now, at the finish, the handle should come right into your abdomen. Legs straight. Your body is leaning back slightly. Slower back up to the catch on the recovery. This is your rest."

"How long do you want me to do this?" I was already breathing hard.

"About twenty minutes, then we'll go up to the workout room and do some weights, and maybe the treadmill. Eventually, you'll be able to erg for an hour or more, easily."

"I bet it feels differently with the oars, in the water."

"Oh yes. The oars are square when dropped into the water at the drive, and then feathered over the water on the recovery. You have to keep your hands loose to make this change, so no death grip on the handle, please. All the while, you are pushing the oars into the oar locks with your thumbs. You get some really attractive calluses from rowing."

The difference between Christine's teaching style, and Ginny's, was painfully obvious. Christine had a matter of fact, direct approach to instruction, as opposed to Ginny's manipulative, hidden agenda maneuvering. I felt a give and take flow of energy in this new team effort. No signs of psychic suck here.

"When are the boats back in the water in the spring?" I asked.

"The Masters and Juniors start as soon as the ice melts, but we hold off the novices until May. The water's warmer." She grinned. "Less chance of hypothermia if you flip your boat. You'll sign a waiver of liability before you get on the water."

"Good to know. Thanks."

Afton's massage studio was attached to her little house near the Norwalk Harbor. She had me sit in a chair near the massage table, while she dimmed the lights. The walls were painted the color of moss, the windows covered with deep brown shades, and a huge drum was sitting in the far corner. A CD of drumming with rattles, and the occasional whistling noise, was playing softly. Sage was smoldering in a stone dish.

"Shamanism is the ability to see in the dark," she explained. "It is not a religion, but instead the most ancient of all methods of meditation, upon which all the religions of the world are based. If you accept that each of us is a descendant of tribal people who revered Nature, this makes sense. The practice allows us to enter the realms of the unseen for guidance, with help from whatever beings you believe exist: angels, masters and spirits of the Upper World, and plants and animals of the Lower World. We are all connected.

"Most religions require intermediaries; men and women in robes, who claim to have special powers and communication with the Great Spirit. In contrast, Shamanism teaches that every person has the ability to do this on his or her own, and that each of us is powerful. We are able to learn from the earth, so that we are grounded, and from the heavens, or Upper World, which is more ethereal."

I nodded that I understood. The sage and the drumming were

beginning to affect me. Suddenly I was riding Joy toward a fence, and hearing a repetition of the main rule of jumping in cadence with her hoof beats: eyes up, heels down.

"Shamans are healers," Afton continued. "You will find that there are remarkable similarities between Western and Eastern beliefs. Working with your luminous field, or aura, I can determine your emotional, spiritual, and physical issues, and help you to heal yourself. Shall we begin?"

She had me stand up, while she walked around me, the palms of her hands facing me, about twelve inches from my body.

"You are in a period of major transition," she said. "You have had a very difficult time, but you are healing. You have been afraid, but you are conquering your fear, and honoring your true self."

"I have recently left my husband, and have filed for divorce."

"That explains it. You are very powerful, and open to evolving, and expanding your luminous field. You have a great capacity for happiness and peace. You find harmony in Nature, and with animals, especially large animals. I'm being shown a vision of a rose, which is the symbol of femininity, and the flower with the highest vibration.

"You are open, but I am also sensing stress. Your right shoulder is tight; I see red in that part of your field. You've had some problems with digestion. You are a light sleeper. We will work on these areas. You've told me that you've had extensive experience with Reiki. You will take a more active role in Shamanic healing. First I want to teach you the breathing."

She showed me the 'fire' breath, which simulated a bellows, and then directed me to the massage table. As with my Reiki sessions, I was covered with a blanket, and a small bean bag was placed over my eyes. The volume of the drumming was turned up.

Afton began to move around me, chanting. She addressed the four directions, east, north, west, and south. She honored the birds and animals of the earth, and the sky above. She addressed the spirit realm, and she called for their assistance in healing 'our sister.' She asked me to bring up my fears regarding the divorce, using the fire breath. I heard and felt various things: she shook a rattle and banged the drum, a candle shone near my face, and was removed. I felt feathers whisking away the energy across my body. There was a whiff of cedar. I was aware and I was able to move my body, but I felt as though I had left Connecticut, and was transported to the Southwest, but hundreds of years ago. There was a sensation of a crowd around me. And then silence.

"I'll be back in a few minutes," Afton whispered. "Take your time getting into the chair."

I slowly returned to Norwalk in the twenty-first century.

When Afton came in, holding a glass of water, I was again sitting down.

"How do you feel?" she asked, holding out the glass.

I considered. "Very relaxed," I reported. "Serene."

"Good. I like working with you." She smiled. "You move energy very quickly."

"Is that what you were doing, with the feathers?"

"Yes. All the bells and whistles are meant to shift the consciousness to the unseen, and to move the energy; break it up and get it out. Now you are more open to peace." She said. "I had a vision of your circulatory system, flowing fast and powerfully. The colors were amazing. I saw purple and gold, and green, the color of healing.

"Consider gathering items of Nature that call you: shells, rocks, feathers; and place them in a place of reverence. A sunny window sill, perhaps, or on your mantel. Really examine each piece. Feel it with your eyes closed, even draw it. See what it says to you."

"I've already started to do that! I like to walk on the beach with my terrier, and pick up shells. You're very psychic, aren't you?" I asked. "But you don't just announce your conclusions. You use them to heal."

Afton shrugged. "Some people are linear in their thinking. They like a psychic to tell them their life. Shamanic healers help you figure it out for yourself, and they guide you to self heal. That takes courage, which you have. Tremendous courage. It is an honor to work with you. You're here to make big changes, and to help women and children."

"I'm all for that," I replied. "But why does the transition have to be so difficult? Last year was a horror of pain and confusion for me, and terrible betrayal. I feel that I almost didn't make it."

"They say that a shaman must experience great personal upheaval in order to achieve a higher level of awareness, and the compassion to help others. You have to heal yourself, before you can help the world. The key is to ask for help. It will always come."

"Thank you Afton, this experience has been eye-opening, to say the least."

"Come back any time. I'd love to tell you about shamanic journeying, and soul retrieval. Please do some reading. And drink plenty of water."

On my way home, I stopped at the book store and ordered every title written by Sandra Ingerman and Michael Harner.

That night I dreamed of Ginny in her home in Westport. The big house is set up like a dorm, or perhaps a low security prison. Instead of walls, there are glassed in openings, like museum exhibits. The furniture is mass produced and the carpets are worn. Everywhere is a sense of drab neglect and shabbiness. There are no doors, and a sensor buzzes each time someone moves from room to room. The bathrooms are grimy, and there is no privacy. I don't recognize anyone but Ginny. She is holding hands with a little girl, who looks just like her. They are both miserable.

Denise and I held our monthly office meeting in the conference room. My assistant, Annie, and Lori, Denise's paralegal, joined us. Annie had brought us ice coffee and muffins.

Denise had her lap top fired up, and a spread sheet in front of her.

"We're doing very well," she announced. "In fact, we are approaching the state of too busy, which can be dangerous. I'm still closing up a few of my files from my old firm in Hartford. The *Garraty* accident case is my top priority. The partner in charge of it, George Gardner, is overwhelmed, so I've asked one of the associates there to help me with the file part time. She lives in the Danbury area, so the commute isn't a problem for her. You'll remember her from law school, Em. She was on the Journal with you. Victoria Marshall."

I threw down my cranberry orange muffin in dismay. "Vicky! Oh God, Denise!"

Denise was startled. "I don't know her well, but she seems nice. They cut her hours, so I thought I'd do her a favor. Why? What's wrong with her?"

"Complete lack of character, for a start."

"What?"

"I told you about Vicky, Denise! She was the one with the DEMERITS!"

"Oh right. The editor."

As lowly second year students on the Law Journal, we had been friends. In our third year, Vicky was elected Editor-in-Chief, and I was elected Managing Editor. First and second in command. Then, she initiated her disciplinary policy. Too many years in Catholic school had taken their toll.

"She ran three second years right off the staff with her control nonsense. She nearly ran me off."

Denise relaxed. "Look Em, that was what? Sixteen years ago?"

"She can't have changed that much, Denise. The woman is a sneak and a liar."

"Well, I liked her. What harm can she be, sitting in the conference room doing research and writing all day?" Denise looked at me. I could tell that she was uncomfortable with the fact that Annie and Lori were witnessing this conversation. I took a deep breath and brought it down a notch.

"OK. We agreed that old files were to be kept out of the partnership, and I'm honoring that. Just promise me that you'll keep an eye on her." I glanced at the other two ladies. "All of you."

"Deal. Now what's new on your agenda?"

"I've got the grandparent custody case, *Palmer*, heating up, plus several divorce mediations, a civil mediation over property lines— some interesting adverse possession issues there, and hopefully a new marital mediation coming in. They haven't signed the retainer agreement yet, so I'm crossing my fingers."

Annie buzzed me right after lunch.

"The state police just called."

Which of my clients had been naughty this time?

"The Palmers are at Disney World. With the children."

"Did the father give them permission to take the kids?"

"Apparently not."

"That's kidnapping!"

"Exactly the term that the police used just now."

I scrambled to find the Palmer's file. I punched Bill Palmer's cell number. Where had I put my antacid pills?

"Emma. I know what you're going to say." Bill sounded panicky.

I suddenly remembered to breathe, and instantly felt better.

"What were you thinking, Bill?" I asked calmly. "How could you possibly take your grandchildren a thousand miles away from home without consulting their father first? Especially with this case pending?"

"Jenny said that she did ask him." Daughter of the Palmers; mother of the kids. "Do you want to speak to her?"

"I can't. She has her own lawyer. You say that she *did* get Larry's permission?"

"For our vacation, yes. But Emma, we want to move here. We've found the most wonderful new community, and...."

"And Jennifer told Larry that you weren't bringing the kids back?"

"She did mention something about enrolling them in school here, yes."

Disaster. "I need to call Rocco. I'll get right back to you."

"I just talked to Roc," Bill said nervously.

"WHAT? He has no business speaking to you. He's your daughter's lawyer!"

"He said you wouldn't mind."

I'll bet he did. "I'll call you right back."

But Rocco wasn't available. "Mr. Fugachi is in court," announced some female from his office. "On a motion to modify custody. Something to do with your clients, the Palmers."

"Excuse me? This matter is in front of a judge, and I wasn't informed?"

"Mr. Fugachi ran into the father's lawyer in the courthouse."

"He never told *me* about it!"

"He's a *very* busy man."

Memo to Self: Add Rocco Fugachi to my (rapidly) growing list of slime ball lawyers in Fairfield County.

Annie buzzed me again. "Mandy Coyle is on the line." The father's attorney.

"Emma, I just wanted to let you know that my *ex parte* motion for custody was denied, but I did get a hearing date set for the twenty-fourth. I've already spoken to Rocco."

I got Bill Palmer in his car. "You need to get back here, Bill. Immediately. Larry is going for sole custody. What were the dates of your reservation?"

"We are supposed to check out on Wednesday, but we'd really like to get the kids enrolled down here."

"That is out of the question. I want all five of you in your car, on your way up to Connecticut, by tomorrow afternoon."

"Have we ruined everything now?" Shaky voice.

"Not necessarily. I'll have to do some backpedaling. Let me know when you're on your way."

Annie came in with a large pile of papers. "This just came over the fax from Bill Palmer. It's so long, he jammed the machine and wiped out the paper. You might want to suggest email next time." She dropped the stack on my desk with a thud. "Oh, and by the way, he's over a month behind with his invoice."

The cover sheet said, in bold letters: "Emma, we have found Nirvana!" What followed was nearly five hundred pages of specs on the new community in Florida, which included a post office, schools, a community pool, and a golf course.

I sighed. Where was my Nirvana?

First thing Thursday morning Bill Palmer called to report that his family had returned to Easton and that both of his grandchildren were back in school. I reminded him of the hearing that was scheduled for the twenty-fourth.

"So you think that we will still go forward, Emma? Rocco Fugachi told Jenny that he thought the hearing would go away."

"When did he say that?"

"Yesterday. She had a meeting with him in his office in the afternoon."

"I don't know. Her ex husband wants to fight for a custody change. His lawyer tells me that Larry feels Jennifer is an unfit mother."

"She is an unfit mother. That's why we're asking for joint custody with Jenny. My wife and I are really the parents. But Fugachi told me…."

"Has he spoken to you *again*?"

"When he called to speak to Jenny. He wanted us to come to the meeting."

"I beg your pardon? He asked you and Jessica to come to a meeting in his office, without informing me?"

"He says that you're the one who is holding up this case. He says that we could come to an agreement without you."

Unbelievable.

"You realize that he said that because I won't let you commit to paying Jennifer's legal fees, don't you?"

"Yes, of course. I knew you wouldn't like this. We didn't go to the meeting." Bill sounded hurt.

"All right. Please don't speak to him again. Tell him I said so, if he tries."

"We won't do anything without talking to you first."

On Friday afternoon Ginny decided to put all the horses through a jump chute.

Lisa and I went into the indoor to help her set up. Ginny's head groom, Gilberto, brought some more jump standards in on the tractor. Short, square, and dark, the man gave me the creeps. He seemed unusually attached to Ginny, and glowered at any one who spoke to her in his presence. Even Lisa, whose focus tended to be on her daughter Sharon's riding, and nothing else, was affected by him.

"Oh, I hope he isn't staying," she whispered, as we hauled jump poles over to where Ginny was pacing out the distances for three jumps. "I don't like the way he only talks to her in Spanish, as though we aren't even here. When Ginny's off the property, he doesn't do any work, and when she drives in, suddenly he's busy."

"And that BMW he drives," I whispered back. "He didn't get that from collecting tips."

"Do you think that they're together?"

"I'd be very surprised," I said emphatically. "But you never know with people."

We built the chute down the right side of the indoor. As Joy was the most experienced, Ginny decided to put her through first.

She was all business in the ring. "We'll start with just poles on the ground to warm her up. If she trots in, she'll be able to squeeze in a nice three strides to the second jump. You understand how to walk a jump line, right?"

"Six feet in, six feet out. Four steps or twelve feet to one stride?"

"Basically. But Joy can stretch out long when she's really cranking, so I'm factoring that in. You can go get her. Her halter's fine. Don't worry about a bit."

I led Joy into the indoor and walked her through the chute in both directions. Joy's eyes looked relaxed, but I was sure that she knew exactly what was going on. "Show them what you can do, gorgeous," I said in her ear. She brushed my cheek with her soft pink and white nose.

"OK, Emma and Lisa, everyone have their lunge whips? I'll stay at the gate end. Emma, I want you at the other end. Lisa, stay in the middle area to keep her going in the correct direction."

"Be careful if she heads for you, Lisa," I said.

"Why?'

"Because Joy can be a real smart-ass," I replied. "She likes to swing in on the side of you that isn't protected. Make sure you flick the whip in both directions. Just don't hit her with it!"

"Thanks for the warning."

"Let her go then, Emma!" Ginny called from the other end of the ring.

I unhooked the lead line from her halter. Joy just stood there, looking at me. I tapped her rump with the whip. Nothing. I snapped the whip in the air. Results. Joy took off at a full gallop, right for Lisa.

Poor Lisa. Joy could smell fear. Lisa waved her whip in Joy's face. Joy stood straight up on her hind end and pulled her front legs up around her ears. I would swear that she was grinning.

"Wave the whip at her, Lisa!" Ginny hollered. But Lisa had had enough. She turned and started to run toward the jump chute. Naturally, Joy followed her.

Time for a little motherly intervention.

I scooted in between Lisa and her tormentor, who was now happily engaging Lisa in a game of cat and mouse around a jump standard.

I cracked the whip near Joy's butt. She immediately executed an impressive one-eighty turn, and scampered off to the nearest corner. I hurried after her, the whip swirling around my head. Joy stood straight up again, curled both her lips back, and hissed at me.

I raced toward her hindquarters, roaring one ferocious GIT! and she was off. Lisa, having recovered, was prepared this time, and we were successful in maneuvering Joy to Ginny's end of the chute. Joy cantered through it a few times, jumping over the ground poles as if they were monsters. Then she settled down, and we were able to start building the fences.

Joy was voice trained. Once we got her into a no-nonsense work-ing mode, we put down our whips and Ginny shouted instructions at her. She trotted into the line and cantered a nice, quiet three strides to the second jump. We had her do this in both directions and then Ginny made the fence at the gate end into an oxer—a double jump. She set the height at four feet and called for Joy to come through again.

Joy loved oxers, and she loved to show off.

I could tell by the look on her face that this was going to be entertaining, and Joy did not disappoint. She took off at a perfect distance, cleared the six-foot standards by well over a foot, and landed on the correct lead at the other end.

Ginny reacted as if she'd been hit by a bus.

"Did you know that she could do that?" Ginny stammered.

"Yep," I replied, smiling.

"Uh, are you aware of how big a deal it is?"

"Oh sure."

"Er, aren't you worried that she might do that while you're on her back?"

"She has."

"She has!"

"Several times."

Ginny looked a little green. "How do you handle it?"

"I hold my position, keep my eyes up, and my heels down, and trust that Joy knows what she's doing. Sometimes I'm in the air so long, I'm tempted to order beverage service."

"Oh my God!"

Lisa started laughing.

"Joy is a lot of things," I said, "but boring isn't one of them. Always be prepared, is my motto."

Ginny suddenly remembered her trainer role. "Well, let's get her going. I'd like to see her do that again, at the normal height this time."

That night I was relaxing in front of the fire with a new mystery, Abby curled up next to me, when the house line rang.

"Emma? This is Ginny. I hope you're having a nice evening."

A call from a horse trainer after hours is never good. I leaped to the obvious conclusion. "Is Joy all right?"

"She's fine. I'm just calling because we didn't have a chance to talk today." Ginny paused. "I miss talking to you. You're so smart."

My stomach tightened up. What did this young woman want from me?

"Are you there?" She asked, clearly nervous.

"What did you want to talk about?"

"Uh, I was wondering if you are planning to show Joy in the spring. I've been going through the prize lists. My family lets me use an office on the property," she explained, unnecessarily. "I'm very close to my family."

"Well, I don't really know," I replied, feeling nauseous. "With the divorce still pending. I doubt that I can justify the expense, right now."

"OK, that's cool. Just as long as you know that I'm really interested."

I felt a swoop between my ears, and everything started humming.

"Showing can be so isolating," she continued. "Professionals are very competitive. And clients only want you to do your job."

I tried a conversational tack. "True. I make a point never to be friends with clients, unless I already am." Where was this going?

"You can't have a long term relationship with them," she concluded.

I didn't reply.

"Are you coming around to the barn this weekend?" Ginny asked.

"I hope to," I replied, trying to breathe. "I have a lot of work for the divorce to get done."

"Joy is a really great horse," she replied, sounding like a teenager now. "She was amazing today. Well, enjoy your weekend."

"You have a cruel streak," I laughed, trying to be funny.

Then she spoke so quietly, I could barely hear her. "They do it to me," Ginny said. "They're cruel to me."

I woke up with a start at two thirty am. Ginny's voice was in my head: I love you, Emma, she said. I know you do, I replied.

CHAPTER FIVE

Vicky

My new lawyer, Donald Hall, had a reputation for representing men in divorce cases, and giving wives a hard time on the stand. Six foot two, with green eyes, dark wavy hair, and a James Bond physique, he was known to be a womanizer. Don had been married and divorced three times, and he owned a forty foot sailboat that he had christened The Seductress. He also had a sign on his office door which read: If it Floats, Flies, or Fucks, it's Going to Give You Trouble.

I thought that Judge Colger-Smyth would be putty in his hands. I was wrong.

At the call of the short calendar, Denise marked our motions ready, and then announced to the judge that Don would be taking over the file. I was watching Nick and his idiot lawyer as she did this. They both registered dismay, and I laughed to myself. They would not be prepared for our arguments, having wasted time assuming that I would cling to Denise as my attorney.

The judge heard several agreements, and one uncontested divorce, and then called our case to come forward.

Don started with our Motion for Temporary Alimony, and put

Nick on the stand. Nick was sworn in by the clerk. Judge Aimée Colger-Smyth turned her head to look at him, and then flushed.

Don began to cross-examine Nick regarding our joint tax return for the previous year. I knew where he was headed. Nick had taken the taxable income number from the return, plugged it into the divorce financial affidavit as his gross income, and then proceeded to deduct his expenses from there. He was, in effect, lying to the court to the tune of thousands of dollars.

"I see that you have deducted your wife's start-up costs for her new law practice as a loss," Don said.

"Yes."

"I see also that you have deducted both of your cars as a business expense."

"Yes."

"How often do you use the Volvo station wagon for business?"

"I don't know, once in a while." Nick growled. "My CPA did the return."

"Isn't it true, sir, that you were once a Superior Court Judge?"

"Correct."

"And isn't it also true that you have sat on the family bench?"

Mike McAfee leapt to his feet. "Objection, your honor."

"I have a right to point out to the Court that the Defendant is very well aware of the rules regarding the filling out of financial affidavits, your honor," Don replied.

Colger-Smyth looked angry. "Objection sustained. Stick to the numbers, counselor."

Denise and I looked at each other. This was a blatant attempt to protect Nick. The fact that he had been a judge in family court was both relevant, and probative of his intention to mislead the Court as to our financial picture in our divorce.

"She's covering for him," Denise whispered.

"I'm worried that they all will," I replied. "The judges in this courthouse are a tight bunch of old school buddies. The concept of fairness is a joke."

Don recovered quickly. He took Nick through each one of his deductions. Nick's answers became increasingly abrupt. It was clear that he was avoiding direct responses. Don lost his temper, and the judge admonished him. Nick looked smug.

Finally, Don, having recalculated Nick's deductions, produced the evidence that Nick had misrepresented his income to the court by nearly two hundred thousand dollars.

There was a moment of silence. Judge Colger-Smyth stood up. "I want to see both attorneys in chambers," she announced, and tottered out the door in her high heels.

Five minutes later, Don came out and waved Denise and me into the nearest conference room. He actually looked apologetic.

"The judge is disqualifying herself from this file, Em," he reported. "The good news is that we have scared her off the bench. The bad news however, is that it will be another three or four weeks until they can import an impartial judge to hear this case. You'll get your money though. I've never seen such a huge financial disparity between spouses."

I fought back tears. Two wasted hearings. Thousands of dollars in legal fees, plus time away from the office. And worst of all, the stress.

Denise squeezed my arm. "At least we've gotten rid of Aimée," she said. "A judge from another Judicial District won't be so caught up in Nick's glow of legal magnificence."

Don rubbed his nose. "Damn, he's an arrogant son of a bitch," Don snarled. "I've never lost my temper with an adverse witness before, not in twenty-five years. He's brutal."

"Yes," I replied, now resigned to waiting until after Christmas for my alimony to kick in. "The judge never should have taken this case from the beginning. There was such an obvious conflict, and she's wasted so much bloody time. I feel like filing a grievance against her."

"Whatever you want," Don agreed. "Just do my blood pressure a favor and wait until after you're divorced."

I just made it to my appointment with my new hairdressers in Fairfield that afternoon. The place was like a factory. Similar to my experience in the courthouse, clients were herded in and out of rooms on a conveyor belt schedule. I was handed a black cape and shown to a line of sinks and chairs. A male assistant of about fifty-five appeared behind me, yanked my head back, and began spraying my upper person with chilly water. He then proceeded to scrub my hair in a manner reminiscent of hosing sheep at shearing time. By the time I got to Melody's cutting station, I was an emotional disaster area.

"Oh I know about Joe," she shrugged. "Everyone complains."

"Then why is he still here?" I asked, a definite growl in my voice. "He's horrible! My horse gets better treatment than that!"

"He's the owner's boyfriend, so no one will say anything to her about him." Carlie gave me a tight lipped smile in the mirror. "Same style as before, dear?"

My sister Kate tried to talk me into coming to her home in New Canaan for Christmas.

"You can't spend the holidays alone, Em. Don't be ridiculous!"

"First of all, I won't be alone, I'll have Abby. Second, I'm looking forward to doing exactly as I please for the holiday season, for the first time in my life. Third, why on earth do you suppose that I would subject myself to Audrey's mouth, in the midst of my divorce drama?"

"But Christmas is for family!" Kate wailed. "Hannah will miss you. I'll miss you."

"Define family, Katherine. You've got your husband and your daughter to buffer you from our dear mother, so don't pretend that you're worried about me. I've got enough on my plate as it is. I'm planning a quiet walk on the beach with Abby, plenty of old movies, and at least two bottles of good sparkling wine. I'll go to the club and work out on Christmas Eve, and then I'll bring Joy's gifts to the barn. It will be lovely."

"Fine, I give up. But please consider being with us for New Year's Eve."

"Only if you can pawn Audrey off on her boyfriend," I replied, firmly. "This year starts my personal embargo on all psychic sucks, and that includes family."

I stopped at Gilder's in New Canaan to pick up some Christmas presents for Joy. Gilder's was a destination for horse people in the Tri State area. The store was beautifully decorated in red, gold, and green for the holiday season, and there were cups of red mulled wine and a cheese platter placed by the counter for the customers. I usually stuffed a stocking for Joy and hung it by her stall. This year she was receiving peppermint bit wipes, a stiff hoof brush, a massager, and some molasses treats. Natalie rang up my purchases, and asked about Joy.

"I hear you're working with Ginny Sherman," she said, handing me the bag.

I took a sip of mulled wine. "Who told you that?" I asked, carefully.

"Oh Ginny was in the other day with some blanket repairs." Natalie reported. "She said some nice things about you and Joy. She said that it's so obvious that Joy loves you, and that she really takes care of you over jumps."

"Did she? That was sweet of her." I let curiosity get the best of me. "Do you know Ginny well?"

"Oh yes! She's wonderful!" Natalie gushed. "She's a terrific trainer, and such a lovely person. She helped me with my Thoroughbred last year. I wish I could afford her—I'd still be at her barn if I could. Ginny is *so* talented, and kind. You'd never know that she comes from such a wealthy, and influential family."

"No," I admitted. "She's pretty down to earth, you're right." I popped one more piece of Camembert in to my mouth. "Thanks, Natalie. Have a lovely holiday."

I hurried to my car, and got out of New Canaan as fast as I could. For some reason, I didn't like the thought of Ginny exchanging opinions with the Gilder's staff. I felt extremely uncomfortable, and more determined than ever to move Joy off the Hunt Fields property as soon as possible.

Denise and I held our office Christmas party the last Friday before Christmas Eve. Dottie and Eliot from our Book Club arrived bearing a huge Williams-Sonoma basket between them. Donald Hall breezed in with a case of chardonnay, and my client Bill Palmer had sent his regrets, and some cheese.

Vicky Marshall, Denise's new associate from her old firm, sailed in, an hour late, empty handed.

I heard a thin voice located almost beneath me say: "How nice to see you again, Emma."

"Vicky. You haven't changed at all." I was being sincere. She was still tiny, blond, and lipless. "Denise tells me that you're working on the *Garraty* file for her."

"Mostly interrogatories," she replied. "And going through the medical records. I used to be a nurse, remember?"

Ah yes. I vaguely recalled a story about a patient who tried to strangle her. Or was that her first husband?

"I was down in D.C. with Justin for a few years after we graduated, but he just got a position with an anesthesiology group in New Haven, so I returned to practice here in Connecticut."

Oh good. "What did you do in D.C.?"

"The same kind of thing. I moved around a bit." The old, evasive look flashed across her face. "I'm very happy to be back in New England."

"So you found her," Denise's voice said, from behind me. "I thought Emma would be somewhere between the caviar and the smoked salmon. Emma, Vicky has been a wonderful help with managing Sonia Garraty for me."

I murmured something polite and excused myself, heading for the punch bowl. I snatched my assistant Annie from the grasp of an elderly male client and pulled up by the copier.

"All right, Annie. How is Vicky behaving? Details."

"Too early for a full report. She hasn't been here much. So far she's been keeping to herself in the conference room, working on her laptop. Seems harmless. What is your deal with Vicky anyway?"

"Let's just say that my stomach did a back flip just now, when I heard her voice, after over fifteen years. I've learned to listen to strong reactions like that."

Annie tossed back her glass of champagne, and reached for another. "OK, I have her in my sights. No worries."

Donald sauntered up, and filled a cup of punch for me. He was clearly three sheets to the wind.

"Here you are, kiddo," he burbled, kissing me on the cheek. "You look really great tonight in that purple dress. Regal, in fact."

This was classic Don behavior, and I didn't let it faze me. "Thanks. Are you getting enough to eat?"

"Sure am." He winked. "I could make a meal of you, right now." He steadied himself, winked again, and moved on to fresh prey. Yuck. Do men really ever think that women want to be spoken to that way? Offensive, repulsive, degrading. Never flattering. But it must work, or they wouldn't continue to behave like orangutans.

Denise and I met over the pastry tray. "Vicky's been great with organizing all the doctor's reports for the *Garraty* case, Emma." She took a big bite of baklava. "As a former nurse, she understands all the medical jargon. She explains it all so well in her memos."

"Terrific."

"She's got the defense's experts' depos beautifully summarized and indexed."

"*What* a valuable asset she is."

"That's what I've been trying to tell you! George and I are extremely pleased with our decision to keep her on this file."

At eight o'clock we started to clean up after our guests. "Make sure you get your mail, Emma," Lori reminded me. "I put it on your desk."

There was a pile of the usual notices from the courts on various cases, and letters from several legal publications, encouraging me to spend money. A few Christmas cards. One had a particularly beautiful engraved cover of snow laden holly trees. I opened it.

Wishing you the loveliest of holiday seasons, it said, in gold calligraphy. Below that was written in a girlish curly hand: Hoping to spend more time with you soon. Thanks again for the gift certificate, and the cookies. Delicious! Always, Ginny.

I sat in my Audi with the motor running. *Grandma Got Run Over By a Reindeer* was playing on the radio.

Always? Who signs a card like that? Answer: Lovers.

Family and friends end notes with "Much love" or "XO", or "Love you!"

Colleagues and business associates usually understand the boundaries of language, and close with "Best regards", or "All best", or "Very truly yours."

What was Ginny to me? Someone I had known for barely two months. I paid her to help me with my horse. We rarely saw each other without at least one equine between us. I had never so much as had a cup of tea with her.

So why was it that I became so unglued whenever she crossed the line from business to personal? Was I attracted to her? *Was* I a lesbian?

I tossed for most of the night. Finally I turned the light back on, and picked up the novel I was reading. But I couldn't concentrate. Abby groaned, stretched, and abandoned me for the guest room.

I sent my memory back, way back, to grade school days, when little girls in the bathroom were curious about each others' bodies. I had always assumed that this behavior was part of normal child development.

When I'd tried to talk to Denise about it after the Christmas party, what she had said was astonishing: "You're such a sensual person Em. I could honestly see you going either way."

I had never been in such a state of confusion in my life. Aside from the fact that it was a tremendous shock to question one's sexuality after more than forty years, I couldn't come up with a decisive answer. I had never been attracted to a woman before. I still wasn't certain that I was attracted to this particular woman.

What was so special about Ginny?

On Christmas Eve at five o'clock, I lit a fire, popped the cork on some very dry sparkling wine, put out the cheese and cocktail shrimp, and watched one of my favorite movies: *Something's Gotta Give* with Diane Keaton and Jack Nicholson. Keaton's part was an uptight, neurotic Broadway author, who fell for her daughter's ridiculously older boyfriend, played by Nicholson. The comedic timing was brilliant, but the real lesson was the transformation that each of them experienced as Keaton's character dropped her defenses, and released her need to control, and Nicholson's Harry learned that he could love a woman over thirty.

When the movie was over, I turned off the lamps, and watched the tree lights reflect on the ceiling, as a few of the big colored bulbs flashed red, green, gold and blue.

A year ago, I was still in Warwick, living with Nick, and practicing law in a dead-end partnership in Fairfield. I was suffering through what turned out to be my last Christmas of putting on a happy face for his nightmare offspring, enduring my mother's vituperative comments, and drinking too much.

Now I was in my own space, surrounded by my own personal items, and blissfully relaxed in the knowledge that from this time forth, my life was going to be whatever I chose to make it.

The Shamanic books I'd been reading claimed that to achieve inner peace, we must feel gratitude.

I glanced around the cozy room, done in my favorite color scheme of blues and greens; at the built in bookshelves filled with a collection of almost thirty years, the brass candlesticks, photos of Joy in big silver frames, and the velvety fur and triangular ears of Abby's head, asleep in my lap.

I felt it—that deeply satisfying sense of gratitude which does not come from ownership of things, but rather from something somewhere inside. Perhaps it was safety. Perhaps it was knowledge that one can enjoy each moment, without revisiting the past, or worrying about the future. Afton was right. Happiness really was all about living in the present.

On Christmas Day, Abby tore through her bag of gourmet dog treats, and played hockey with her new stuffed hedgehog. I opened the three packages that I had under the tree: Kate's amethyst earrings, a horseshoe bracelet from her daughter Hannah, and a crystal butterfly from Marilyn, my Reiki Master. "Butterflies are the symbol of profound transformation," she had written. "I'm so proud of all your hard work. You are a courageous woman, and a leader."

I put Abby in her winter coat, and we walked down to the beach. There were a couple of inches of bright white snow on the ground, but the temperature was barely freezing, and the sun was strong. We sat on the jetty and watched the tide come in, sniffing the wood smoke. All of the large homes around us were burning wood fires, and mixed with the salt air, and the sound of the surf, the effect was intoxicating. Reverence for Nature, Afton had said. Find your balance in Nature. Shamanism was the most ancient of all methods of meditation.

But how does one meditate? Prayer was asking the question, one of the books had informed me, and meditation was waiting quietly for the answer. Quiet the mind. How on earth did I do that?

Breathe.

Be still.

With my boots planted in the sand, and my terrier lying on the rock next to me, I slowed my breathing and centered my focus on the horizon line. If a thought tried to break through, I visualized it vanishing on a cloud.

Answers. Use your experiences to help other women who are too afraid to help themselves. How? And then a swirling of ideas came through. Create a team of professional women, in various careers, all committed to supporting women through life transitions. Divorce, retirement, widowhood, job relocations, family challenges.

I saw a website. And butterflies.

Then a gull squawked, Abby jumped up, and the connection was broken. But I had gotten what I wanted. If I had to suffer through this divorce nonsense, at least I could put the agony to good use.

Two days after Christmas, I took Denise out to breakfast and pitched my idea to her.

"Give me examples of the kinds of professionals that you mean." Denise said, spearing her western omelet. "Lawyers and therapists, obviously, but who else?"

"Investment advisors, tax accountants, financial planners, mortgage specialists. Think about how many times you've had to clean up a garbage separation agreement because the lawyers who drafted it didn't have a clue about finance."

"Too many times, you're right. Housewives are awarded homes that they can't afford, or agree to secure mortgages that they aren't qualified for. It's pathetic. These people don't do their homework."

"Exactly. We gather a group of like minded female professionals, and set up a web site. The site provides the public with all manner of useful information. We write articles within our areas of expertise, and post them; give talks at local libraries. Do radio interviews. We can offer the members an excellent referral source, and the public benefits as well."

"But we wouldn't be pro bono, right? Our practice is doing better than I expected, but we really don't have the team, or the wherewithal, to take on freebies right now."

"No pro bono. We'll leave the question of fees to each individual member."

"There has to be a disclaimer on the web site."

"Agreed. Otherwise, it looks as if we're practicing law with non members of the Bar." I ordered a second ice coffee. "Do you know a good female CPA?"

"Yes, and two financial planners. Rita Nelson is just down the Post Road in Westport."

"I'll get going on some of the therapists I know. There's a terrific investment advisor in town, and I've worked with the people at Warwick Mortgage. We'll touch base after the first of the year. What do you think about calling this group the Connecticut Affiliation of Professional Women?"

"Good. It makes it clear that we're not a formal entity."

"The last thing I need is another lawsuit on my hands. You know what people in the midst of personal drama are like."

"Their problems are always someone else's fault?" Denise grinned, buttering her toast. "And they'd rather start a war, than look at themselves? I'm all for helping people, but I never forget that CYA is the name of the game."

CHAPTER 6

First Battle Won

The day before New Year's Eve, I decided that I needed a change of scene. I put some food in a small cooler for Abby and me, packed my camera and my painting kit in a Bean tote, and spent the day on a driving tour of Litchfield County. Located in the Northwest corner of the state, Litchfield is Connecticut at its best; the region is noted for the natural beauty of its farms, country back roads, pristine lakes, and small town colonial charm. With the exception of a few cases pending in the courthouse, located on the green in the Town of Litchfield, I had almost no experience of this part of my home state.

I drove north on 95, merging on to Route 8 outside Bridgeport. I watched as the crowded landscape of Fairfield County fell away, and was replaced by snow covered hills and thick groves of trees for miles.

I was listening to a CD of one of my favorite Agatha Christie mysteries: *Towards Zero*. The psychology of the plot was fascinating; Christie described "zero hour" as the final result; the murder. But the action of everything coming together at that point required months, even years in the planning. The players, the circumstances, and even the weather—it all affected the ultimate outcome.

My research claimed that there was no such thing as coincidence. All that happened to us had been perfectly synchronized, just as it was supposed to occur.

Therefore, my marriage to Nick, my decision to open my own practice with Denise, my move, and even meeting Ginny, a woman who was challenging what I thought was rock solid in terms of my sexual preference—all of these blips on my life radar—they were planned and played out for my benefit, and for those of every other member of the cast. So that we might evolve into the people we're supposed to be.

There were always tests along the roadmap, Afton had explained, like a gauntlet. "Most people don't have the courage to make big changes," she said. "They prefer to stay on the hamster wheel, going round and round the same way, year after year, wondering why they're so miserable. The therapists pump them up on happy pills, and nothing ever is resolved. Do you know what's so impressive about you? If something isn't working, you keep making changes until it is. That's really rare, and truly inspiring."

"What happens to those people who don't do the work?" I asked, thinking of Nick.

"They have to come back in another life, and try again," Afton had replied.

I resolved to get it all done in this life. Enough.

I exited Route 8, and headed west on 118 into the Town of Litchfield. On the right was the quintessential white Congregational Church with tall steeple; on the left, the perfect town green. Magnificent old homes and ancient trees lined the streets, and West Street beckoned with a cluster of restaurants and shops.

I could feel the beginnings of Nirvana.

Abby and I parked, and took a stroll along the paths of the snow covered green, past the museum and the courthouse, looking briefly into the kitchen shop. A West Highland White Terrier in front of a real estate agency sniffed noses with Abby, who wagged her tail in friendly reply.

I sat on a snow free bench, while Abby devoured a few bone shaped treats.

According to the shamanic books I'd been reading, misery was created when one gave up one's power to another. Living a lie resulted in stress. If we didn't listen to our bodies, and honor what we truly felt, we became ill. Sickness may manifest at any level, from acne, grinding teeth, and headaches, in my case, to debilitating mental and physical 'dis-ease,' and even life threatening conditions. Doctors kept people coming back for heavier prescriptions, more tests, invasive procedures, racking up the medical bills, when the problem always stemmed from our emotions.

How this theory applied if one's child fell out of a tree, I wasn't clear. At least orthopedic specialists had a reason for being. Perhaps illness and accident came in two separate categories. Afton would probably say that there were no accidents.

Abby and I walked back to the car, and I consulted my map. If we headed west on 202, we could check out several bodies of water in the region: Bantam Lake, Mount Tom Pond, and Lake Washington.

As we moved slowly down the hill from Litchfield into Bantam, the change in architecture and zoning was immediate. The houses became smaller, the businesses more commercial. Bantam Lake was big, with a North Bay and South Bay. The 209 side of the water was almost entirely commercial. There were several beaches at various points, including the Litchfield and Morris town beaches, and a public campsite. This was a motor boater's domain in the summer months. Mount Tom Pond, in contrast, was a small, no motor-craft lake, which was part of a state park. There were a few small houses scattered around its periphery. It had the atmosphere of a Boy Scout Camp.

I continued west on 202. We entered the town of Washington. I took a left on 47 into the center of the town. It was as if I had time traveled back to eighteenth century Connecticut. Here was perfect harmony between land and architecture; beautiful old farm houses, set for centuries in rolling pastures, and outlined by low fieldstone walls. Horses grazing on hay dotted the view. There was a pervasive feeling of peace, and stability.

From a practical standpoint, there was also a market, a library, an art center, home supply stores, and a few gourmet delis. Remoteness was wonderful, but I'd had enough of twenty minute drives to the grocery store in New Hampshire.

The temperature was warming up as we approached lunch hour. Abby and I turned around and headed north on 47, back to 202 west, and took a right on 45 into the historic village of Bridge Hollow, on the edge of Lake Washington.

Suddenly, I was home.

I had been missing the Pequot Lake house in New Hampshire, which Nick had brought into the marriage, and would retain when the divorce was final. It was his life, his history, and nothing to do with me.

This stunning body of water more than made up for it.

Several towns in Litchfield County bordered on Lake Washington. Abby and I drove past gorgeous properties, some right on the lake, some across the road, with matching boat houses on the water. Two venerable inns, famous for their excellent dining, were part of the terrain. At the state park, I left the Audi in the lot, and Abby and I ate our lunch on one of the picnic tables, overlooking the beach, with the public campground to the right. We had this part of the lake to ourselves. I loved the concept that everyone had the right to enjoy this exquisite place.

I visualized Abby and myself launching my kayak from here when the weather got warm.

Then I began to visualize life in a home here, as Marilyn and Afton had taught me.

I saw a gray shingled gabled house with white trim, similar to the one I was renting in Southport, only bigger. I saw porches and fireplaces, and a big kitchen with lots of space for guests to mingle. There were built-in bookshelves all around the living area, two window seats, and lots of overstuffed chairs. I created white bead board, and local art on the walls, hard wood floors, and several cheerful guest rooms. Bathrooms in white tile, with big tubs, and double showers. A master bedroom with a fieldstone fireplace, windows on three sides; colors in blue, green and white. There was air and light in every room. French doors led outside to a slate patio, with a lawn down to the water's edge, and a dock to launch my rowing shell. The feeling was of relaxation, and unhurried pleasure.

I attempted to visualize a life partner for myself, and could not. I knew that there were too many questions to be answered first.

I pulled my sketchbook out of my art bag and drew the shoreline of the state park. The tall grasses were reddish brown in the January cold, but there was beauty in the stark landscape, and a few robins pecked the ground along the frozen shore.

A state park employee stopped by to say hello, and Abby was gracious as he offered her a treat from his pocket. He said that he was originally from New York, but now lived in Thomaston, and was a contractor by trade; he also plowed driveways in the winter to earn extra money. "We've been up here for eleven years," he said, "and we love it. It's a slower way of life, and you can't beat the scenery."

Abby and I returned to Southport at dinner time. There was a message from my friend Laura on the house line voicemail: *"Hi Emma. I know we haven't spoken for a while, and I hope everything went smoothly with the move. Would you please give me a call when you have a chance?"*

We met for lunch the next day. "It's Reg," she began, with a shell shocked look on her face. "We've been dating since the fall, and we can only get together on weekends, because he lives in the city."

"What's wrong?"

"Last weekend I was staying at his place, and we decided to work out at his gym. We were in the free weights room, and I happened to be chatting with the guy next to me. Reg got up, stood right in front of us with his arms crossed, and glared at this James, the entire time we were talking. James eventually left, and when we got back to Reg's apartment, I tried to talk to him about it. He said that I had been completely disrespectful to him, and that I had made him look foolish at his own gym. His face suddenly twisted into something really frightening, Em. I can't describe it. I could feel waves of his anger hitting me. When I tried to leave, he took my purse, which meant I didn't have my car keys, or my wallet or cell phone."

"Oh my God! Did he hurt you?"

"He wrenched my wrist pretty hard, getting the bag away from me. I felt trapped."

"You *were* trapped Laura. There's no other word for it. How did you finally get home?"

"I couldn't leave all day. We ate in, and I had to spend the night with him. It was horrible—I was so afraid. The next morning, I left while he was still asleep." She paused, looking miserable. "He's been calling me ever since."

"Please tell me that you haven't picked up."

"I don't. I just want him to go away. I'm afraid that this will come out in the divorce. Steve is so bitter. And that's not all, Emma. I think Reg is dealing drugs."

I remembered not to judge. "How long have you suspected this?"

"Since our second date, from some conversations that he had on his cell. I know what you're going to say."

"Why did you keep going out with him, Laura? You're an accomplished, well educated, terrific woman. Why would you subject yourself to such a dangerous person, at such an intimate level?"

She sighed. "He made me feel so special. He said all the right things, told me how elegant and beautiful I am. He took me to plays, and some very nice restaurants. Our first date was a lovely dinner cruise around the island. I guess I just enjoyed the attention. Looking back, we really didn't talk much. I always felt a little lonely around him, as if I wanted to cry, without knowing the reason."

"It sounds as though your gut was warning you, but you didn't listen."

"What should I do?"

"You should formally end it, just in case there's a problem later. But don't inflame him. Perhaps you should send an email—tell him that the travel is too taxing for you, for example, and that you don't want to continue to see him. Make sure you print a copy, and save it. And definitely save any emails that he sends back to you."

Laura swallowed. "You're expecting trouble."

"I'm hoping that the fifty miles distance from Manhattan will minimize the revenge, but keep me posted, whatever happens."

"I promise to listen to my inner voice, Em, from now on."

"Don't beat yourself up too much. We've all been in denial about relationships at one point or another. How else could I have tolerated over a decade with Nick?"

They say that third time's the charm. It certainly was regarding my temporary alimony award.

The Honorable Lauren Milo had just transferred into Ludlow Superior Court to take over the Family Division. Tall and athletic, and originally trained, as I was, in civil jury matters, she had already terrified most of the Matrimonial Bar. By the end of our hearing, I wanted to name my first born child after her.

We started the hearing all over again. Nick and his oafish counsel Mike McAfee had had the foresight to correct Nick's financial affidavit, but the Judge wasn't fooled.

After tolerating testimony from both sides, she awarded me ten thousand dollars a month as temporary alimony, retroactive to the time of the aborted hearing with Judge Colger-Smyth. She also ordered Nick to reinstate his life insurance policy with me as beneficiary. Finally, she ordered him to re draft his will, leaving the bulk of our estate to me.

Bless the woman.

"See Em, the system still works," Donald Hall said happily at lunch. "You were great on the stand, by the way."

"Thanks. That idiot Nick hired wouldn't know how to frame a question if his life depended on it, so it wasn't that tough."

"Yeah that was a bad move, trying to show that you make plenty of money on your own now, but that you never did a thing during the marriage. That moron McAfee was trying the case, instead of focusing on the issue of temporary alimony." Don smirked. "And he *really* didn't like hearing that you had a right to continue the lifestyle that you both enjoyed during the marriage. Then he made the big blunder of bringing up Nick's health, after the judge had entered her orders. She blew him off pretty sharply, I must say. Is your husband sick?"

"Not physically, as far as I know."

"Huh. Well, I'll make a note to ask him at his deposition. And you were right—they did bring up the value of your horse."

I grinned. "Nick hasn't figured out that he can't push my buttons with Joy any more. It's all he's got. I didn't cheat, and I'm not addicted to anything."

"What were they trying to prove? Your marriage broke down because you rode your horse too much? That you could sell her, and live on the proceeds?"

I rolled my eyes. "I think he's just throwing anything against the wall, trying to get me to crack. He's going to fail miserably. Nick is obviously driving the bus on their team."

Don signaled for the bill. "Always a mistake, as you know. People who are getting divorced are functioning on pure emotion—whether it's fear, anger, revenge, or a combination of all three. Nick is giving himself very bad advice. He's going to pay for it."

"We both are. What's our date for the Special Masters again?"

"Mid-April. There's plenty of time. We may get a trial date as early as September."

"My discovery is in, not that I had much, so we're just waiting for Nick to produce the documents that you've asked for. I feel like I can relax, for a bit, anyway."

Don took the last bite of his burger, and a swig of beer. "You're all set for the time being. Work on building your practice, ride your horse, paint your pictures. Let me deal with Dumb and Dumber."

More money coming in meant that I could breathe better. I told Lisa the good news in the tack room the following evening.

"What if he doesn't send you the check every month?" Lisa worried.

"Nick's a member of the Connecticut Bar, remember, and a former Superior Court judge. He won't risk his platinum reputation by being in contempt of an order of the court."

"I hope you're right." Lisa looked away. "Emma, Jack wants to raise the board at the home farm."

I frowned. Jack had already padded the price when the new barn was completed, and considering that the farm lacked an indoor, or a trainer, they were already asking more than the average. "To what?" I asked, trying to keep the dismay out of my voice.

"To sixteen hundred a month." I must have looked shocked, because Lisa continued quickly, "we feel this is fair. After all, we offer all day turnout, and more shavings than most places."

I didn't respond to such ridiculous reasoning. There were barns in the area that charged half of what Lisa was suggesting, with all day turnout, and adequate bedding in the stalls. I knew that I couldn't justify this kind of expense with the divorce pending. And I knew without question that Lisa wouldn't back me up if I challenged Jack.

"We're offering discounts to our other boarders, as they have more than one horse each, but as you have only Joy…." Her voice trailed off. "Well, I just wanted you to know."

"Thanks Lisa," I said, swallowing hard. "I guess I'm going to have to start looking for a new home for Joy." Inwardly, I was shocked. Lisa and I had always been friendly, if not close. This sudden disregard for my well-being, especially in the midst of my divorce, was very disturbing. Where was this change of attitude coming from?

"If that's your decision, of course." Lisa closed her trunk, and turned to leave. "Sharon really likes working with Ginny, and they talk on the phone at night quite a bit. Ginny has agreed to drive in to our farm to work with Sharon and Wally, once we go back in the spring. I'm so pleased."

And she left.

Annie buzzed just before lunch. "Attorney Fugachi's holding for you."

"Emma! I've been trying to reach you for days!"

"I've been here, Rocco. To whom did you speak?"

"What are we doing on Monday? Are we still going forward?"

"Absolutely. There have been too many unnecessary delays in this case. The grandparents have a right to intervene."

"My client doesn't want her parents involved."

"But she's perfectly happy to have my clients raise the children at their expense?"

"I thought we were working together on this case."

"We were, until I found out that you are appearing before a judge on this matter without notifying me."

"The husband's lawyer said she'd call you."

"It isn't Mandy's job as opposing counsel to let me know her every move. It *was* your job, as we were supposedly *working together.*"

"What about the custody evaluation?"

"I'm pressing that as well. Your client is a flake and an absentee mother. I want that report produced, and I want a guardian *ad litem* appointed for the kids."

"Are you going to let the grandparents agree to pay my bill?"

"No damn way. It's a conflict of interest, and you know it. And if I find out that you've been speaking to my clients without my permission again, I'll take you straight to the Grievance Committee."

"Nice. I guess I'll see you on Monday then."

I slammed the receiver down. Worm. At least I could fight against the zero character, good ole boys on this playing field, if not in my own divorce.

CHAPTER SEVEN

CAPW

The first meeting of the Connecticut Affiliation of Professional Women was held in Warwick, at the office of Warwick Mortgage.

Denise and I, as the new Co-Chairs, sat at the head of the conference table. We'd come up with an agenda, and as everyone networked over bagged lunch from 12:30 to one pm, I went over my pitch. Twelve professional women from various parts of Fairfield County had shown up to hear our ideas.

Having promised that everyone would be out the door by two, I started the meeting promptly at one o'clock.

"Thanks to all of you for coming today, and a special thank-you to Carol for booking her conference room for our use." Carol Porto, president of Warwick Mortgage, smiled graciously. "Denise has passed out a copy of today's agenda to each of you. First, we would like to propose a mission statement, which encompasses our reasons for starting this group, and our goals for the future."

Denise read from her notes: "We are an affiliation of professional women, experienced, compassionate, and committed to supporting individuals during major life transitions such as divorce, retirement, widowhood, career changes, or family challenges.

Our mission is to provide a holistic approach that will help dispel myths, alleviate fears, and empower clients through education."

"Denise and I feel that we want to be open to female professionals who are on board with our mission," I continued. "We are not just looking for another business networking group. While we are not offering pro bono services, we do want education of the public to be our primary focus. Any questions so far?"

"Are we extending our expertise to men as well?" Liz Klein, a career coach in Fairfield asked. "Many of my clients are men."

"Of course," Denise replied. "Emma and I both feel that our philosophy should be that the more men learn, the better it is for both sexes."

"Excellent approach," Randy Pollack, Ph.D. replied. "It's the separation of the masculine and feminine that created most of this planet's problems. It's time to bring the two halves back together."

"What about group funds?" Tracy O'Brien, a CPA in Norwalk, asked. "How much will it cost to join, and who will be the treasurer?"

"We thought that for now, we'd charge each member one hundred dollars to join." Denise replied. "Benefits will include a bio and contact link on our website, and the option to post events and articles on the site. Furthermore, we've found an excellent PR person, so she will generate a press release in the new member's papers of choice, and any internet marketing, as well."

"We'll keep the funds in our firm trustee account for the time being," I added, "until or unless we elect a Treasurer to take over. We've considered meeting every month to six weeks, at locations to be announced. A suggestion would be to have a member speak for each meeting, after conclusion of business. Perhaps we might occasionally bring in outside speakers. Again, the goal is to educate, and empower the public, as they navigate difficult life transitions."

"I'd be happy to speak at the next meeting," Rita Nelson, a

financial planner and investment advisor in Westport volunteered. "Very few people understand what my work entails."

"I've always felt that I'd like to give something back," Nan Richardson, a trusts and estates attorney in New Canaan said, "and I know several libraries which encourage offering free talks to the public."

"To whom do I write the check?" Jean Corbett asked. "Here's my card, by the way. I handle life, health, and disability insurance, and my office is in Darien."

"Carbury and Frederickson, Trustees," Denise replied, distributing our firm cards as well. I gathered up all of the checks. "Emma and I are interviewing two or three web designers who want to take on this job. Obviously, the group site will be our best face to the public, so we want it to be a polished product."

"And unless anyone objects," I said, "we've decided that our logo will be the butterfly. It's such a powerful symbol of transformation."

"That was incredible!" Denise said on the drive back to Westport. "You could really feel the positive energy in the room. I can't believe that such a new group is already in the black with fourteen hundred dollars. You did a terrific job explaining what we're all about."

"Thanks! It just felt right. And I bet you that most of those women have been through some tough time or other, and wished they had a group like this to lean on. It's a terrific resource from every standpoint."

"The public gets what they need, and the members get the networking."

"Yes. And I love that we're not excluding men."

"So did that psychologist from Westport. What was her name? Randy? She seemed like a hot ticket. I know you don't approve of therapists, Em, but she impressed me."

"I liked Randy too. She asked me to have lunch next week. She has an interesting case that she'd like to refer to us."

"Good. She's just down the street, near your rowing club. Well, I had better get going on the website. We should be up and running soon." Denise pulled into our parking lot. "This is a positive step for your divorce, too."

"Because it looks like I'm really working hard on building our practice and getting my name out there?"

"That, and the fact that you've emerged from Nick's shadow. You'll be a force in your own right." Denise laughed. "I'll have the web guy tag you as our group Founder. That always looks intimidating."

Annie looked in. "Bill Palmer wants to talk to you. Are you here?"

"Emma, there's been a development."

"Enlighten me."

"My daughter has switched sides."

"Sorry?"

"Jennifer is now siding with her ex husband against her mother and me."

"I guess she wasn't happy with the judge's decision to let you in the case."

"More than that. She's decided that the Family Relations officer, *and* the guardian *ad litem*, are totally biased against her."

"That explains Jennifer's agenda. What about her ex husband?"

"I take it that things didn't go too well for Larry at the FRO either. Jenny says that Attorney Fugachi is drafting an agreement between them. He has no intention of informing you. Or the guardian *ad litem*."

"Let me take care of Fugachi. I'll call the GAL. This is ridiculous. Jennifer had to know that you'd be telling me about this."

"I think the prospect of getting my goat was so enticing, she didn't think clearly."

"Well, forewarned is forearmed, as the saying goes. Thanks Bill."

All of my shopping trips to Williams-Sonoma the previous fall had convinced me that I needed some cooking instruction. The Westport store offered free classes on Sunday mornings, before normal opening hours. I decided to attend the next demonstration, the theme of which was stews.

The sales ladies had set up the shop as a classroom for the event. About thirty women, and a few men, received their recipe folders, and walked by the counter, looking attentive. A large blond woman, a local caterer, was chopping vegetables. She had a selection of chef's tools laid out carefully on a towel.

"Do you mind if I ask you about your knives?" I inquired. "I've always heard that a true cook has the best cutting equipment, but I don't know a thing about them."

"I like Wüsthof," she replied. "Their Classic series is my favorite. The balance and control are excellent, the handles are comfortable, and you get the very sharp, strong steel blade." She handed me a large chef's knife. "Try cutting this onion."

It was awkward, until I was shown the proper technique. "I'll be teaching a class here in two weeks on slicing and chopping," she announced, producing a copy of the schedule. "Why don't you come? These skills are really fundamental if one wants to cook well."

She called the group to order. "My name is Hilary Webster. I'm a CIA graduate, and I've offered catering here in lower Fairfield County for nearly ten years. Today we're going to learn about making stock from scratch, and some easy stew recipes."

Hilary took us through the differences between store bought broths, which were usually full of salt, and a sample of her own homemade stocks, in both beef and chicken. Hilary's efforts were clearly superior; the flavors were intense, and there wasn't a hint of salt, or chemicals. "The aromatic vegetables are celery, carrots, and onions. With the help of some fresh herbs the result is wonderful. The stock freezes easily, as well. I'm sure that you've all heard about the benefits of organic produce and meats. Buying organic is healthier, and it improves the taste of your food. Being aware of what you eat, and where it comes from, has never been more important."

At the end of the class, I bought a twelve piece set of Wüsthof Classic in a hardwood block, and a cook book on twenty minute stews. I stopped by to thank Hilary, who was ladling out samples to customers.

She smiled at my big bag of professional knives. "Good for you. Make sure that you sharpen them often," she advised. "Or they will lose their edges. I look forward to seeing you at my next demonstration. Perhaps you'd like to help?"

I resolved to do more research on food and its energy. There had to be a basis for the old saying: "You are what you eat."

CHAPTER EIGHT

Randy

Lori, Denise's assistant, and our office manager, appeared at my door. She looked angry. "The Palmers have left, Emma."

"Left? As in left the State of Connecticut?"

"Yes. I just got off the phone with Rocco Fugachi's secretary. Bill and his wife packed up their daughter and the two kids and moved to Florida on Saturday."

"Did the father know ahead of time?"

"They all knew ahead of time, apparently. The daughter promised Fugachi that he would get paid, but the secretary says that they're not holding their breath over the outstanding balance."

"What about our invoice?"

"There's still a balance of just over ten thousand dollars. Could we sue them in Florida?"

"Pretty tough. We don't even know where they are. Even if we did, we'd have to hire a Florida lawyer to bring the action, and there's still no guarantee that the Palmers have the wherewithal to pay the judgment."

"I tried Bill Palmer's cell phone number. Naturally, it's no longer in service."

"No. I'm sure he left with all his bases covered."

"But you got the grandparents everything that they wanted! Residency with the kids, joint decision making power with the parents. You convinced the judge to let them in the case in the first place."

"Welcome to family law, Lori! This is why domestic attorneys get such big retainers. Clients who are in emotional turmoil are not thinking rationally, and they're certainly not thinking that all the calls they make to their lawyers, and all the motions that they want heard are on the clock."

Lori looked disgusted. "It certainly explains why you and Denise want to blow off litigation, and just take mediation cases. All that hard work! Well, maybe we can write off the loss."

Write off the loss. Nick always said that no good deed goes unpunished.

To my chagrin, Rocco Fugachi had been hired to represent Angela Caxton's husband in their divorce. I took several deep cleansing breaths before walking into the family courtroom in Devon Superior Court. Whatever happens, don't deck him, I kept reminding myself.

Angela was sitting in the front row, looking stunning in a green Dior suit. "Which one's your husband?" I whispered.

"That's Dick. The long haired tweedy professor in the jury box."

"He's not supposed to be sitting in front of the bar. The judge will have a fit."

The Honorable Judith Tuchman was finishing up her short calendar docket. "Which file are you here on, counselor?" She asked, directing her question to Dick Caxton.

"I'm waiting for my lawyer," replied Dick, looking bored.

I could have told him his mistake right off the bat. "STAND

WHEN YOU ADDRESS THE COURT!" Her Eminence hollered. Dick scrambled to his feet. "Take a seat behind the bar. AND GET YOUR HANDS OUT OF YOUR POCKETS!"

"I'm really enjoying this so far, Em," Angela said.

I stood up. "Emma Carbury, your honor. We're here on *Caxton v. Caxton*."

The clerk handed the judge the court file. "Where's Attorney Fugachi?" Her Worship inquired.

"Here, Judge." Rocco strolled in, his round face and bald head shining with perspiration, a bulging briefcase in each hand. "I had three other matters in courtroom two."

"So kind of you to join us. I'll see counsel on the *Caxton* case in my chambers in five minutes."

"All rise!" The Marshal bellowed. The judge got up from the bench and made her exit.

Fugachi slithered over to Dick and motioned to follow him out into the hall. I glanced at the clock.

"What are they doing?" Angela asked.

"Probably swearing Dick to a revised financial affidavit," I replied. "I threatened to blow the horn. Your husband's last affidavit was total garbage."

"What's going to happen today?"

"Step one is to get rid of their motion for exclusive possession of your house, which never should have been filed. Step two is to get Dick out of your house, and you back in. You understand that Judge Tuchman won't be able to hear this case if your divorce goes to trial, right?"

"Because she will have talked about the file with you in chambers?"

"Correct. When the jury is the finder of fact, say in a car accident, or a med mal case, it doesn't matter what the lawyers say to the judge in camera. But in Connecticut, family issues are heard in what's called a court of equity, and the judge is the finder of fact."

Judge Tuchman, de-robed, appeared by the bench. "Now where have the men gotten to, Emma?"

"I believe that they're out in the hall, your honor."

The judge rolled her eyes. "Marshal, will you be so good as to retrieve Attorney Fugachi and his client?"

The clients were asked to remain in the courtroom, as Rocco and I followed the judge back into her chambers.

"Do I have current financials, counselors?"

"I have a new one here, Judge," replied Fugachi, handing over same.

"Do you have a copy for Attorney Carbury?" Judge Tuchman asked.

"My client just signed it, Judge."

"I expect you to be prepared when you come into my courtroom, counselor. You know better than this." She picked up the phone. "Gina, would you make a couple of copies for me in the secretaries' office?"

The clerk came in, secured the affidavit, flashed me an amused grin, and withdrew. "Now that you've finished delaying this conference, Attorney Fugachi, let's get down to business. What does your client want at the end of the day?"

"Mr. Caxton wants alimony and health insurance for five years, and half the house. He also wants a percentage of Mrs. Caxton's pension."

"Attorney Carbury?"

"The parties have been married for six years, your honor. The house was left to my client by her parents, and she has been solely responsible for its maintenance, insurance, and taxes for over ten years. Mr. Caxton has earned almost nothing during the course of the marriage, although in the past he has been employed as both a college professor, and a magazine journalist. He has refused two offers from prestigious institutions in the last year. Furthermore, he has been nominated for a Pulitzer, twice. He is only twelve years older than this wife and more than capable of supporting himself."

"How's his health?"

"Fine, Judge," Fugachi replied.

"Then what's this man's problem? What does he do all day? He's not home raising the kids, right?"

"There are no children in this marriage, your honor."

"So did they agree that he would stay at home and vacuum the rugs?"

"No, your honor. The cause of the breakdown, from my client's perspective, is that as soon as her journalism career began to take off, her husband decided he wanted to take a vacation from the work force. My client was never on board with this decision."

"He's writing a book, Judge."

"For six years?"

"It's going slowly, he says, Judge."

"I'll bet it is. I think I've got the picture. What about this motion for exclusive possession, Attorney Fugachi?"

"The man needs a place to live, Judge."

"The man needs to get off his butt and obtain employment, counselor. If this motion had come before me on short calendar, I would have denied it from the bench. Any of the judges would have done the same. Tell your client that he has thirty days to either accept one of those previous offers, if they are still open, or to find alternative opportunities elsewhere. He is to vacate the house within thirty days as well. We're going back in the court-room, and this is going on the record as an order of the court."

The clerk returned with copies of Dick Caxton's financial affidavit.

"Gina, buzz the court reporter, will you? We're ready." The judge got up and put on her robe. "I'm marking this on my calendar, Attorney Fugachi. Thirty days."

"OK Judge."

"And take your hands out of those pockets."

Angela and I had lunch at a diner in Devon. "Thanks Emma! That was so quick!"

"You're welcome, but all I did was give Tuchman the facts. She had a pretty nasty divorce herself a couple of years ago. Her husband was a sponge as well."

"Aha. That's why you wanted the Honorable Judith to hear our motions."

"Absolutely. She's also one of the few judges in Fairfield County who won't put up with Rocco Fugachi's slimeball tactics. It's refreshing to watch her in action. With most of the male judges, I feel like I'm fighting alone against the old boys' club. They all cover for each other. You'd never know that it's the twenty-first century."

"So Dick has to be out, and employed, in a month? What if he blows her off? She could put him in jail, couldn't she?"

"Yes, but she has to find that he is in willful contempt of court first. Don't worry, we'll fix things for you."

I met Randy Pollack, Ph.D. at the Riverside Tavern for lunch the next day. The hostess brought me to our table by the water. Randy, who had already been seated, was a tall, handsome brunette, with warm hazel eyes, and amazing cheekbones. She had a turquoise silk scarf wrapped around her neck, and a large silver and turquoise bracelet on her left wrist. Beaded feather earrings hung from her ears. She radiated power.

"Cherokee," she said, laughing. "I rarely tell people, but for some reason I feel comfortable with you."

"Are you a shaman as well as a therapist?" I asked, a little stunned. Why hadn't I seen Randy as a medicine woman when we met earlier?

She flinched. "I'm uncomfortable with calling myself a shaman. It feels dishonorable to my ancestors. I prefer the terms shamanic practitioner, or healer. But yes, I do ceremonies for clients; individual, and groups."

We ordered our cobb salads. I described my work with Afton, and the research that I'd been doing. Randy made some additional reading suggestions, and reported a recent misadventure with a sweat lodge, where a participant had collapsed and nearly died.

"It's obviously vital that only people who have been carefully trained should be doing this kind of work," she concluded. "You can't just buy a drum and hang up a shaman shingle. Please be careful."

I promised that I would. "Tell me about the case that you want to send to my firm. Is it a divorce?"

Randy shook her head. "Post judgment. My patient is the husband. He's a state police officer, and seemingly a very devoted father to their one son, Max, who is just turning thirteen."

"Who has custody?"

"The parents have equal decision making power, and the boy, unfortunately, is living in a split residence arrangement."

"Oh dear."

Randy nodded. "I understand the reasoning behind the order, especially as the parties live only two blocks from each other in Trumbull. From the father's perspective, the mother is smothering the boy. She reacts to him as though he's still a toddler. She coddles him to the point that she won't allow him to do anything on his own. He drinks out of a baby's sippy cup, and he sleeps in the same bed with her."

I raised my eyebrows. "Is there any indication of incestuous behavior? A teenage boy in bed with his mother is worrisome."

"I've read the article that you wrote about incest under Connecticut law. It's why I want to send this patient to you. The residency issues have to be sorted out, and soon." Randy passed me the bread. "If what the father is telling me is true, then this is a case of incest."

"Have you had the mother come in as well?"

"No. She refuses to attend a session with me. She is willing to get help for Max however, but the parents can't agree on a therapist. From what the father says, I feel that he is probably over compensating for Max's lack of masculine influence at his mother's. He's too tough on the boy."

I sighed. "So it's a stalemate?"

"Yes, and that always means bringing in lawyers, as you know."

As I ate my lunch, I considered bringing up the Ginny scenario. I wanted a professional opinion, and as Randy had a foot in each camp, so to speak, I thought she was the perfect candidate for some good solid advice.

"That poor angel!" Randy exclaimed, when I had outlined the story for her. "I have nothing against having money, far from it, but the very wealthy do seem to operate on a level of cruelty that is all their own. They have so much power, and they know how to manipulate the system."

"But the law is the same," I said firmly. "The trick is to find lawyers and judges who aren't influenced by the deep pocket citizens. What will happen to Ginny?"

Randy leaned forward. "It depends on her inner strength, ultimately. It's obvious that she's been the victim of severe childhood trauma. The perpetrator could be anyone—probably a relative. If Ginny has the proper support, she can fight her family, who will no doubt do anything to pay her off and keep her quiet. She would have to commit to do the work—energy and therapy. If not, well. The drugs are just a bandage. In my experience, the terrible pain catches up with the patient eventually, and she can't live with it. It could mean hospitalization, or worse."

I put down my fork. "Is there anything I can do to help?"

"Only if she asks for assistance, and even if she does, be careful. The dreams and the telepathy indicate to me that you may be the only person that she trusts, which places a huge burden on you. Get her to a qualified professional as soon as possible. Incest survivors have been betrayed on the most horrible level—by people that the child victim trusts and loves, and who are supposed to be loving her back. Like a trapped animal, she will attack if the old feelings of terror are triggered. Go slowly, tread lightly, and above all else, watch your back." Randy reached into her purse and handed me a few of her business cards. "Call me if you need me. I can help your friend."

CHAPTER NINE

Telepathy

My Book Club reconvened the following week. Angela, as our new member, had offered her huge old house in Ridgefield, and dinner in her library. I picked up Jane in Warwick, and we drove north together.

"How are you doing Emma?" Jane asked. "Your face is much brighter than when I saw you before Christmas. Are you beginning to enjoy your freedom?"

I let out a long breath. "Yes, finally. You never really understand how it feels to be in prison, until you escape. I now realize that I spent over ten years bracing myself against the force of Nick's selfishness and control, and how abusive and destructive it all was. I can see that our fighting had become like a poison in the house. There is no tension in my new home."

Jane was thoughtful. "My parents never fought. I was raised to believe that if a couple argued, then the marriage was over. Pete, on the other hand, grew up in a family where everyone said what they thought at the top of their lungs, regardless of the consequences." She sighed. "After forty years, I still haven't adjusted to his behavior."

"That's why I'm enjoying my new life. I'm completely free of emotional obligations to anyone. Best of all, I spent the holidays alone with Abby, and it was heaven. For the first time since I became an adult, the new year has arrived, and I felt excited to meet it."

Jane looked at me, and was silent.

Angela had inherited her parents' beautiful old home on historic Main Street in Ridgefield. I turned the Audi onto the semi-circular drive. Eliot and Denise pulled up behind me. Angela had ordered a catered, four-course Italian meal. Dottie arrived while the antipasto was being served.

"We're celebrating the fact that I am finally back in my own home," our hostess said happily.

Jane brought out her copy of *Franklin and Winston* just as the pastry platter made its appearance. One of the waiters fired up the cappuccino machine.

"I suggest that we begin our discussion, lest we all slip into a pasta-induced semi-consciousness. Excellent, by the way, Angela. Thank you very much."

Eliot attempted a hearty affirmation to that sentiment, but managed, instead, an impressive belch.

"Having said that," Jane continued, "we are here to consider a beautifully written portrait of a friendship between two extraordinary men."

"A relationship that affected world events in a time of great crisis," Dottie added.

"Shall we compare the two leaders? Dorothy, what did you make of Jon Meacham's assessment of Roosevelt?"

"Honestly? I felt that FDR did not measure up. He came off as the shmoozy, superficial politician who held all the cards. It was a little upsetting."

"Because we were all taught as children to revere Roosevelt?"

"Partly that. But also because Americans are trained to imagine that we are the best at everything."

"What about you Angela?"

"I agree with Dottie, but on different grounds. If we were to lay the professional resumes of the two men side-by-side, what conclusions would we draw?"

"Churchill won the Nobel Prize for Literature; he was a military hero and an accomplished orator and artist. He stood alone with the Brits against Hitler for years before the U.S. was forced to enter the war at the end of 1941. He was probably the greatest leader of the modern world." Dottie looked around at us. "What did Roosevelt do?"

"He collected stamps," Eliot replied.

"Oh come on!" Denise was clearly annoyed. "What about twelve years and four elections to the White House? What about the Depression, and Prohibition? Except for the Civil War, this country has not seen tougher times, and FDR was a strong leader and a brilliant political strategist to the very end. I've always thought that it's terribly sad that he didn't live to enjoy our victory."

"So have I," I admitted. "Especially as it was probably the pressure of the job that finally killed him."

"Let's get back to the relationship between these two great men," Jane urged. "How did it evolve? They first met in London back in 1918. Neither made a positive first impression on the other."

"They didn't come together again until their famous meeting aboard the *Augusta* off Newfoundland in August 1941," I remarked, turning to the photograph of Roosevelt and Churchill, singing hymns together aboard the HMS *Prince of Wales*.

"The Lend-Lease program was already in effect by then," added Angela.

"Yes. The Americans were helping with the war effort; if not with the actual fighting. Of course, Pearl Harbor changed that."

"I'll bet that FDR enjoyed his superior position in the relation-ship," Dottie remarked. "He would never have wanted to be in Churchill's vulnerable spot."

"Alone, under attack, and desperately needing aid?" I replied, with feeling. "Nobody would. Most likely, Roosevelt felt that way inside, though, every day. He *was* confined to a wheelchair for more than twenty years."

"What, if anything, was a turning point in their friendship?" Jane asked.

"Tobruk." Denise said.

"Definitely," Angela added. "Rommel humiliated the British in North Africa. Meacham quotes Churchill: 'Defeat is one thing; disgrace is another.' Churchill received the news while visiting the White House, from FDR himself. Churchill was, by all accounts, devastated by the surrender of his generals to the Germans."

"Roosevelt immediately offered American support with his famous line: 'What can we do to help?' The answer was Sherman tanks to the Middle East." Denise said.

"What I wouldn't do for some large artillery now and then!" Eliot laughed.

"But the tanks made all the difference later, in El Alamein," Denise argued. "It was a turning point in the war. The Germans were forced out of the oil region, which meant a huge victory for the Allies."

"Query whether the same support would have materialized had Churchill been in London at the time Tobruk fell, and his request to the Americans for aid had been made through the usual chan-nels," Dottie said.

"You're right," I replied. "It's all about personal relationships, isn't it? Complete understanding of, and compassion toward the other person's agenda. Eleanor Roosevelt said that often enough. Not that I've ever agreed with what my husband calls her Socialist politics—I believe in less government, not more—but her hands-on, humanitarian approach to every aspect of American policy was probably the approach that saved North Africa during the war."

"Because Franklin was right there to witness Winston's personal despair, and reacted immediately to it."

"Yes."

"That analysis will segue beautifully into my next question," Jane said. "What happened when Stalin became the third wheel in this alliance of powerful men?"

I thought about what Dr. Foyle had said about psychic vampires on a global scale, but did not reply.

"FDR switched sides," Eliot announced.

"Not politically, perhaps," Angela responded carefully. "But he did appear to enjoy leaving Churchill as the odd man out."

"It was reminiscent of prep school cruelty," added Dorothy. "The boy with the least means got aced out."

"But think about Emma's point," Jane said. "Isn't it possible that FDR deemed that this was the best approach to enlisting Stalin's support? There were trust issues, remember. The Russians had signed a pact with Germany. Stalin's country had been invaded by the Nazis." Jane paused. "It was clearly FDR's strategy to woo Stalin with the personal touch."

"Well, if that's true, the President certainly didn't share his scheme with his pal Winston before trying it out," Eliot remarked.

"But Franklin Roosevelt liked secrets," Angela said. "He learned the fine art of prevarication at a young age. His mother was the domineering matron type, and his childhood practice of dodge and weave became the foundation of his approach to politics."

"Exactly," I said. "You should all read *Sara and Eleanor* by Jan Pottker, for a very clear picture of what went on within the triangle of FDR, SDR, and ER. How Franklin managed Sara was the key to everything he did in later life. Never give anything away; send them off thinking that they've gained something."

"When they haven't," Angela finished for me. "It's a wonder that any one person ever felt really close to the man."

"How could they?" Dottie asked. "He always wore a mask."

"Was he really a friend to Churchill, then?" Denise said. "Or was that just more political management?"

"Excellent question," Jane replied. "What kind of a man was Winston Churchill?"

"Instead of an overbearing and adoring mother, he had an over critical father and a completely uninvolved mother," I said, turning back to the beginning of the book. "Churchill's youngest daughter, Lady Soames, described them as pretty awful parents."

"So, while Franklin evolved into a man who was emotionally distant, Winston was always looking for love and approval," Jane concluded. "This probably explains the suitor like methods that Winston employed to win Roosevelt."

"But in the end, after so many trips across the pond to visit FDR at the White House or Hyde Park, Winston did not go to Franklin's funeral."

"Yes," Jane said. "Why was that, do you suppose?"

"A reaction to the nonsense with Stalin?" Dottie offered.

"The courtship was over," Eliot volunteered. "So Winston didn't bother."

"But were they friends?" Denise asked again.

"I think so," Angela said. "Each after his own fashion. There seemed to be much affection in the letters and cables that they sent to each other."

"I agree," I added. "Men do not define friendship and intimacy as we do, remember. They value different things."

"And every relationship is riddled with conflict and disappoint-ment. Everyone has boundaries." Denise said.

"Like the betrayal that Eleanor felt when she arrived in Warm Springs and found that Lucy had been with Franklin at the end?" Eliot asked scornfully.

"Yes," Denise replied. "Just like that. I have come to the realization that it is impossible for one person to be all things to another person. We each need variation in our lives—intimate contacts, diverse avenues to inspire us. Or we die inside."

"Good gracious Denise! I hope you never say that to your husband!" Jane exclaimed.

"I don't know," Angela said thoughtfully. "Maybe it's the journalist in me, but the longer I'm on this planet, the more I question what we were all taught that was deemed to be morality. Innumerable black and white rules made up by strangers long ago, that don't necessarily fit into our existences today. Government—and organized religion—have a lot of ignorance to answer for."

I agreed. "After many years of family litigation, I can honestly report that there is no such thing as normal."

"Absolutely," Angela said, looking down at the wedding ring that she still wore. "And we can not afford to waste one moment of our lives worrying about someone else's self imposed guidelines. This is not a dress rehearsal, ladies."

On the drive back to Warwick, Jane asked me how the Ginny situation was developing.

"I will definitely be glad when Joy is safe in her new barn, and I can take a breather from all this drama."

"Is Ginny still making you offers, though?"

"Oh yes, but they're always very subtle. Nothing that would ever compromise her in any way. She sent me a Valentine. On the cover were two little girls holding hands and walking away from the viewer, down a country lane. On the inside she had written 'For Emma and Joy, Always from Ginny.' She calls me at night fairly regularly, mostly to chat about the barn, but her conversation is usually accompanied by one or two obvious sexual innuendoes."

"This must be very confusing for you. Have you asked her to stop?"

"No."

Jane frowned. "But I don't understand that, Emma. Clearly this young woman is making you uncomfortable. How does she behave when she's working with your horse?"

"Very professional. Occasionally girlish. There have been rare bursts of flirtation, and she's always looking for reasons to touch me. Ginny is a chameleon in terms of personalities, and very careful that there are no witnesses if she says or does anything out of line. She is intelligent, and an extremely talented horsewoman. She's doing a wonderful job with Joy, and her lessons are helpful. I just don't have the energy to confront her, and frankly, I don't want to. There's been enough upheaval in my life lately."

"Yes, I can see that," Jane said. "I've never been a big fan of confrontation myself. I prefer to keep to the same dance steps, it's less taxing." She paused. "Do you think that you are attracted to this woman?"

I thought about it. "I'm attracted to *something* about her, but I'm not sure what it is. There's a big mystery around her, and you know how I am when it comes to mysteries."

Jane did not laugh. We only spoke again to say our good-byes in Jane's driveway.

That night I dreamed that Ginny and her daughter are standing outside a barn on a big estate by the Long Island Sound. The child is trying to get Ginny's attention, but her mother is cold and inattentive. Both are wearing dark blue. Then suddenly I'm in the kitchen on the estate. I'm looking at little Ginny, while a nanny figure is telling me about Ginny's home life. I am extremely uneasy about this invasion of Ginny's privacy, and I want to leave, but the nanny continues to gossip. "She's very sweet," the nanny says, right in front of the child, referring to her as 'Virginia,' "and she's eager to please. But she's not one of them. Her mother is off the wall." "Who is the father?" I ask, in desperation. The nanny leans forward and whispers: "The grandfather."

On Monday morning, Joy was moved to her new home, Running Fox Farm, in Fairfield. A small private barn, about fifteen minutes from my home, this property met my requirements: all day turn-out, bright, roomy stalls with plenty of shavings, no pressure to show, and a monthly board fee that was half of the amount that Jack and Lisa wanted for almost exactly the same facilities. Joy had a buddy named Peanut; a large gray pony who wouldn't stand for bad manners from her new paddock mate. Best of all, the owner had agreed to long line Joy for two hours a week for a small additional fee. This meant that I was the only person who was riding my horse, but the extra training freed up my time. The relief I felt from this transition was stupendous.

Annie buzzed me at my desk the next morning.

"Your friend Laura is holding for you," she announced. "She sounds like she's losing it."

"Emma! I'm so glad I caught you! I need help!"

"What's wrong?"

"Reg. He threatened to hurt me!" Laura wailed.

"How? On the phone?"

"No. He was waiting in my garage this morning when I left the condo. Right by my car."

"Has he ever pulled anything like this before?"

"Not there. He's been outside my office building a few times in the morning. And he's waited for me in the parking lot at the club. This was the worst, though. He had blocked my car with his."

"Did he have a weapon?"

"No."

I could hear Laura's teeth start to chatter.

"He grabbed the keys out of my hand and pushed me up against the handle on my door. There's a big bruise on my side now. Then, he threatened me."

I took a couple of breaths to control my rage. Assholes like this creep always sent me into warrior mode. "What did he say to you?"

"He said he didn't like that I've been avoiding him. He said that he knows that I've been carrying on with other men. Carrying on! Emma—I haven't been on one date since I broke it off with Reg."

"What you're doing or not doing is immaterial. This jerk is now guilty of assault and stalking. Did you call the police?"

"No, I wanted to talk to you first."

"Did he threaten you?"

Laura started to cry. "He reminded me of how strong he is, and how easy it is to crush a throat. Especially a girl's throat."

I turned to my computer and logged onto the research program. I clicked on to the Connecticut General Statutes. "Here we go, Laura. Section 53a-181c. Stalking in the first degree, which is a Class D felony. I'll bet he's done this to other women, and, if he has, this section applies. If not, we move on to 53a-181d. Stalking in the second degree: Class A misdemeanor. Subsection (a) says the following: A person is guilty of stalking in the second degree when, with intent to cause another person to fear for his physical safety, he willfully and repeatedly follows or lies in wait for such other person and causes such other person to reasonably fear for his physical safety."

"It's a worse offense if he's been nailed for this kind of behavior before," I explained. "Either way, we need to get you a protective order."

"Thanks, Emma."

"No problem. I'll meet you at the Stamford Police Department in half an hour. And we should probably get a digital shot of that bruise."

I decided to do some research on telepathy. The Ginny dreams had escalated to the point where I was getting three or four a week, sometimes two in one night. I'd wake up with a start, look with horror at the luminous dial by my bed, fall back to sleep, only to be woken up just a few hours later with round two. Sometimes there were pictures. Sometimes I only heard Ginny's voice. One night I dreamed that she and I are dancing in a barn with a whole cast of grade school girls, with Ginny's voice-over commentating in my head. Another night, she is living in a drawer. I sneak into her house and rescue her, but she is growing so fast, by the time we get outside to my car she is too big for me to carry.

The most disturbing dream came a few weeks after I had moved Joy. I am hiding in Ginny's bedroom closet. There is a pair of bright white figure skates hanging from a hook on a wall. They are a little girl's size, and clearly they have never been used. The closet door is cracked open, so that I can see into her room. Her father is coming in, and I am terrified. Then the scene switches suddenly. I am in my parents' bedroom. My father is lying in bed, asleep.

I woke up in tears, finally sure of what Ginny had been trying to tell me for months.

The question remained, how could I communicate this discovery to her?

My dream books were helpful. Apparently, we were all telepathic, but most people were too skeptical to acknowledge this fact. They were determined to believe that everything was a 'coincidence'. Therefore, if A was thinking about an old friend from whom she hadn't heard in years, and that afternoon the old friend called, it was just a fluke. If B and C were talking over breakfast and found that they each had exactly the same dream the night before, it was merely the power of suggestion from something that happened the day before. Or if a mother was driving to work and suddenly heard her son calling to her, and then moments later the police informed her that there had been an accident, the occurrence was labeled 'feminine intuition', and dismissed. People would make up any excuse to ignore synchronicities, which were really the Universe sending messages to us.

So how could I use this research to help Ginny?

Finally, I found some practical information. According to one psychic, if you wanted to reach someone in their dreams, think about what you wanted to say just before you fell asleep, and state your intention to send it out to them.

That night, I turned out the lights and lay flat on my back. As I felt sleep come over me, I visualized Ginny's face, and mentally stated my intention to reach her in her dreams. I was brief: "Hi Ginny. I understand. Know that I am here if you need me. I will always be your friend."

CHAPTER 10

Ginny's Story

Ginny left a message on my voice mail the following morning. Her deep voice was shaking, and I could imagine the emotional effort that took her to this step: *"Emma, I'm ready to talk to you. If it's OK, would you meet me at the barn on Monday, say around nine am? The property is closed to boarders on Mondays, so we'll be private. Please text me one way or the other. Thanks."*

Ginny was standing by her car when I pulled up at just a few minutes to nine on Monday morning. I had purposely worn jeans and a sweater, and left my suit hanging in my Audi. I wanted to be there as a friend, not as a lawyer.

As I walked toward her, I got the familiar heavy jolt in my solar plexus. I took a deep breath, and wrapped myself in white light.

"Hey," Ginny said. She pointed towards the paddocks to our right. "Do you want to walk?"

We had to be painstaking, as going along the path was diffi-cult. Constant freezing and thawing all winter, combined with the daily traffic of horses, had left deep icy ruts at regular intervals. As I picked my way, I was careful to create as much space for Ginny as possible. All of my reading had been clear about the way to approach incest survivors, and uninvited touch was taboo. I shouldn't have worried—she bumped into me at nearly every step. She reminded me of a small child, trying to stay close to the grown-up who's with her. I felt her hand brush mine, but I didn't respond. I knew that it was Ginny's way of testing me. I had to maintain a tenuous balance: respect physical boundaries, but don't act repulsed by her at the same time.

"So now that you know," she said suddenly, reading my mind, as usual, "do you feel the same way about me?" She stopped, and looked straight into my face. She was so close, I could see the green gold flecks in her blue eyes.

I didn't hesitate. "I think that you are an extremely intelligent, sensitive young woman, and an amazing horseperson. I also think that you've been through hell."

That must have satisfied her, because we resumed our walk.

"It started when I was still pretty young," Ginny said, not looking at me. Her shoulders were hunched, and her gloved hands were shoved into her pockets. "My dad—he's really my step dad—it's another big lie that I have to tell. Anyway, he would come into my room at night. He said that since I wasn't really his daughter, it was OK. He also said that I couldn't talk about it—it was our secret. I wouldn't be allowed to live there any more if I told."

I remembered to remain calm, and not react to what she was saying, even though my stomach dropped like a rock.

"Did you love him?"

"Yes!" She seemed relieved that this was my first question. "Part of me still does, I guess. Even though now I know what he did was totally wrong, and he could have gone to jail." She looked over at me quickly. "I read your article. A few times."

Utilizing all of the psychological and legal research that I had done for a divorce case last year, I had posted an eleven page piece on incest under Connecticut law on the Alliance website.

"I was hoping that you had," I replied. "What did you think of it?"

"I thought you really nailed what it's like, to feel lower than low, and to have no one to tell about it. The whole secret thing is a big deal," she said, thoughtfully. "You have to live with it for so long, hold on to it. You just don't know any other way. And you feel so ashamed, all the time. You think, maybe it was my fault. Maybe I could have stopped it."

God, this was horrible. "Have you had any therapy, Ginny?" I asked, quietly.

Ginny made a sound like a fake laugh. "I'm on meds for bipolar disorder. Have been for years."

"Does your therapist know about your dad?"

"Nope. He pays her. And I get the pills through his company."

As simple as that. Ginny couldn't bite the hand that fed her, and abused her at the same time. And her psychiatrist wasn't astute enough to figure out the problem on her own. Randy had explained it to me: most therapists were too uncomfortable with incest to deal with it, let alone be trained to detect the signs.

"My business isn't really mine, you know," Ginny said. "It's a family company. One of many with the Halloway Brook umbrella. The name's from the stream that runs through the family estate in Westport."

"Does that present problems for you? The fact that you don't have ultimate say regarding your farm?"

She looked at me with disdain. "Are you kidding? He holds it over my head all the time."

"What is your dad's name?"

"Douglas. Doug. I have to call him Dad when other people are around, but when …I had to call him Doug when we were alone."

I couldn't repress a shudder. Luckily she was looking straight ahead, and didn't catch it.

I took a deep breath. "Is he still coming in to your room at night, Ginny?"

She shook her head. "That pretty much stopped when I went to college." She thought for a moment. "I got pregnant when I was in high school. I was fifteen." Her voice rattled. "He had a doctor friend of his take care of it. Take care of it," she repeated. "Another man I had to spread my legs for. After that, it was less and less. Then I went off to school. I wanted to get as far away as I could."

"How on earth did you get through college? You must have incredible focus."

"Yeah, well. I divide myself up. You know. School, home, riding. I've got lots of different parts."

Randy had explained that trauma victims dissociate to survive. Some become so fragmented that they develop multiple personalities.

"So you graduated what? Eight years ago?" Ginny nodded. "And you've been on the road ever since? Showing horses?"

"Yep. Traveling, going to Europe to meet with breeders and dealers, spending as much of his money as I can. I have a trust fund, but I can't touch it. It's called a 'special needs' trust, or something. I have to talk to a woman at our bank when I need more than my normal allowance."

"As in, when you want to buy a horse?"

"Yes, exactly. Or a new car. Sometimes I go to him. To Dad. Then I yell and scream and carry on until he gives in. I think he's afraid that I'll lose it one day, and tell. I know he's paying me to stay quiet."

What a way to live. Ginny was a hostage in her own family; one who occasionally shook up her captor with threats of a tell-all exposé. She probably fooled herself into believing that these tantrums were exhibitions of rebellion, instead of desperate screams for help. I bet that good ole Doug crossed his fingers at the start of every horse show, hoping that the next jump would be too high; too fast. And at some level, Ginny knew it.

"You wanna hear what the real joke is?" Ginny's blue eyes flashed rage. "He keeps threatening to throw me out on the street, and yet I *know* it's the one thing that he'd never do. He'd never want to lose control over me to someone else. It's all about control." She paused, and clenched her fists. "But for some reason, I still stay. I'm so afraid, all the time."

"Afraid to be on your own?"

"Partly. It's the other thing that your article was dead on about. I have no friends. I'm always worried that I'll screw up and tell. It's easier to side step people and their questions. I've gotten really good at it. I know I'm a little weird. People don't get me, and how can they? I'm living a fake life. I'm a total fraud."

I resisted the urge to hug her. It took every ounce of restraint that I had.

"You're not weird, Ginny. You're suffering from severe, long term trauma. If you were a soldier, they'd call it shell shock."

"Oh!" She looked startled. "So I'm not bipolar?"

Slippery slope. "Look, I'm not a therapist, so this is definitely not my area. But in my opinion, based on nearly two decades in the practice of law—and I've dealt with trauma in car accidents, family problems, and even some assault cases—it's all the same thing. The shrinks paste on every label and sub label under the sun, and pump patients full of every drug that's created, but when the rubber meets the road, all of these people were just plain traumatized."

"That's good," Ginny decided, rather anti-climatically. "Because I sure am tired of being told that I'm crazy."

I handed her Randy's card. "I've mentioned to her that I think you're suffering from childhood trauma. If you feel comfortable, give her a call. Randy is very kind, and very smart. She'll help you out, and she'll answer to no one but you."

Ginny looked suspicious. "Not even you? You two won't talk about me?"

"Not unless you give us your consent, in writing. Confidentiality is sacred, in both our practices."

"OK then. Thanks for this." She glanced at the card briefly, and pushed it into her back pocket. "You won't tell anyone else? Not even Lisa?"

"No one else."

"Thanks," she said again. "Uh, sorry about the night-time stuff. I didn't mean to mess with your sleep. I just didn't know how else to get through to you."

"I admit that this was a new experience for me. I did a lot of research…."

Ginny grinned for the first time. "I'm sure you did!"

I laughed. It felt good to vent some emotion. "And once I realized that everyone is telepathic, I kept working at it, until finally I was able to send, as well as receive."

"Oh, I heard you all right! First time I've ever gotten a message back. You were loud and clear."

"What a shock." We both laughed.

"Why me Ginny?" I asked, a little nervous. "You've been keeping this secret for most of your life. Why me? Why now?"

She thought for a bit. "I really can't answer that. I knew, the second I met you. I just knew I could trust you. That you were strong enough to handle this, and that you wouldn't judge me." She bumped me with her elbow. "I guess I was right, huh?"

"You were absolutely right."

"Well," Ginny said, after a pause. "How about we head back? I have a few horses to ride today."

"Always working, that's you," I joked, not thinking.

Ginny shrugged. "It beats going home."

Driving home I remembered Randy's admonition. "Be careful with her. Sometimes she'll be a savvy athlete and business woman of thirty odd, and sometimes she'll be a terrified little girl. That's the tragedy of childhood abuse that goes untreated. These people are emotionally arrested. Expect two steps backward, for every one step forward. And tread lightly."

I hoped that I had.

Jane sent me a text on April second, inviting me to dinner at the new Spanish restaurant in Westport. She arrived in a beautiful aqua blue wool dress, and a gray cashmere shawl. She kissed me on the cheek, a light fragrance of gardenias about her person. I had a sudden flashback to my grandmother in her sixties.

"I want to celebrate your birthday with you, if a little early," she said, as we looked over the menu. "I've ordered a bottle of sparkling wine." The waiter arrived with the standing ice bucket, and poured us each a glass.

"This is lovely, Jane. Thank you," I said, grateful.

"Here's to a whole new life, one replete with happiness and freedom," she said, touching her flute to mine. "And above all, personal fulfillment."

"Yes please!" I replied, enjoying the wine. We ordered tapas, and Jane passed the bread to me.

"Tell me all about your new law firm," she said. "Are you and Denise pleased with your progress?"

I explained that we were still taking litigation files as we built up our mediation practice, and that we were pleasantly surprised with the speedy surge in business since the fall, when we'd opened our doors.

"We both know so many people, who send us referrals—mostly women—that we haven't had to do any advertising at all. I've read that it's a sign that you're on the right track when everything seamlessly falls into place. I'm meeting new people at the rowing club all the time, and Denise has her kids' friends. There are a lot of unhappy mommies out there!" I spread more tapenade on to my bread. "I like helping people who feel trapped. You spoke of fulfillment just now. It's the reason that I became a lawyer."

"Helping people? Women, do you mean?"

"And children. Kids really are in the most damnable position. They have no rights, no say in anything, and until they are eighteen, a whole line-up of people is making pronouncements about their health, their education, and their activities. If someone who is supposed to be helping them is abusing them instead, the kids are too terrified to speak up. Even if they did, no one would believe them. It's like being in prison," I said, thinking of Ginny. "There is much legislation that needs to be changed, so that homemakers' contributions are valued, and children feel safe. I'd like to become involved in advocacy."

"Thirty years teaching in a public school system has convinced me that it is still a man's world out there," Jane replied, "despite what the feminists claim, and that it is the men who generate most of the money, and therefore, the rules."

"The rest is just smoke and mirrors," I agreed. "It's why Denise and I have started our women's networking group—yes we get great referrals—but the whole point is to empower women through education of the system. We have financial people, accountants, therapists, insurance people, lawyers, career specialists—we're all committed to the team system of getting a woman to reclaim her power and her self esteem."

Jane smiled. "It takes a village to get divorced? I saw your press release in the Norwalk paper, and I read your article on the group website. Impressive. You've certainly given the public a bird's eye view of the Family Bar in Connecticut. I think that you and Denise are doing a wonderful thing for the community."

"Ultimately, I want to branch out into the rest of the state, and then have other states pick up on our momentum. Some of our members are licensed in New York and New Jersey, for example."

Our tapas arrived. "Then I'm sure that you will," Jane replied. "You are a 'can-do' lady, Emma. You have amazing energy, and a great deal to offer any group, or relationship. By the way, how is it going with your friend, the riding teacher?"

I swallowed, and composed myself. "That blew up in my face, I'm afraid."

"How? Did you finally tell her to leave you alone?"

"No," I grimaced. "She told me to back off. I got a certified do not contact letter from her last week, which she carbon copied to her father—alleged father, I should say—telling me that I'd been disrespectful, and I was never to bother her again, or she would 'consult counsel.' She practically accused me of stalking her at her 'place of business,' which is ridiculous, as she invited me to visit her when the barn was closed."

Jane put down her fork and leaned forward. "What do you really think is going on?"

"I think she mouthed off to her step father about my being a lawyer, and wanting to help her, and he threatened her. He probably dictated the letter to her." I fiddled with my napkin. "She made it sound as though I had come on to her. After all those phone calls! I'm so glad that I kept the two cards that she sent me."

"Be careful Emma. This Ginny sounds like someone with serious emotional problems. People like that will turn on you in seconds. Suddenly they are the victim, and you are the aggressor-villain. They will protect their family, and especially the abusive parent, at all costs, and throw you to the lions." Jane sat back, and divided the last of the wine between us. "I've been in your position before. Students practically screaming to me for help, calling me at night, leaving notes on my desk, and then when I tried to step in, I was the bad guy. Now I just refer them to their guidance counselors. I can't handle the craziness. Mental health specialists call it borderline personality disorder."

"I know. My friend Randy is a therapist here in town, and the bulk of her cases are women suffering from the affects of childhood trauma. She explained it to me." Basically, Randy had said run, don't walk, from the Ginny situation. "She'll probably never leave her wealthy family," Randy had predicted. "It's all she knows. She's too damaged and terrified to consider a healthy life away from them. You can't help her, so save yourself from any further sacrifice."

"So that's that." Jane concluded. "I know that you cared for her, Emma, and I'm sorry for your pain. But I'm sure it's for the best. You want nurturing, supportive people around you now. Not someone who would merely suck the soul out of you." She looked down at her large diamond ring.

"Yes," I responded dully. "That's that." Five months of disturbed sleep, and dream analysis, feeling conflicted about my sexuality, discovering that Ginny had been a victim of horrific abuse, intervening even when my lawyer's instinct told me to keep away, and then nothing. A complete waste of emotional energy and time. The Universe certainly moved in mysterious ways.

"It's not the same up at the lake in New Hampshire without you," Jane said cheerfully, with a skillful switch of topics. "I especially miss our walks with Abby and Macduff. Mac was looking a little thin, the last time I saw him. I'm sure he misses you too."

I suddenly wanted to go home. Too much loss was like a rock on my chest.

"I'm hoping that once everything is over, I'll be able to have Mac for overnights and weekends. Like visitation with kids," I laughed, trying to ease the heaviness that I felt.

"I'm sure that he'd love that," Jane said. "Would you care for dessert? They make an excellent flan here."

When I finally returned to my house that night, it was with a sigh of relief. Abby was upstairs, passed out on my bed. She had burrowed in between the pillows, and all I could see was her tawny rump, and the black pads of her hind paws. I scratched her back, just above the tail. She woke with a start, knocking two pillows on to the floor.

"Evening, my precious Abigail," I said, burying my nose in the top of her head, and breathing deeply of Eau de Terrier. She yawned. "Thanks for sticking with me, and being my best friend." With a big sigh, Abby moved over to the tartan blanket at the foot of the bed, and disappeared under it.

As a birthday gift to myself, I decided to stop at Gilder's to buy a new pair of half chaps. The spring line of jackets and shirts was in, and I amused myself by browsing the Burberry display. I picked out a deep blue jacket and tried it on. Perfect. I threw a couple of pairs of socks in my basket, and proceeded to the counter.

Natalie, who had known me for years, and waited on me often, took one look in my direction, and deliberately walked into the stock room. The manager, a jolly Irish woman named Mollie, took care of me. Normally garrulous and friendly, she rang me up without saying a word, and didn't ask about Joy, as she normally did.

I said thank you to her politely, and turned to go. Then a thought struck me. "Mollie—has Ginny Sherman been in the store lately?"

Mollie started visibly. "Just a few days ago. She said that you had left her farm, and that you didn't send Joy back to Lisa's."

"I'll bet she did," I replied. "Take a free legal tip from an experienced trial attorney, Mollie. There's a very good reason why hearsay isn't permitted in court as evidence."

Mollie looked angry. I gave her one of my best professional smiles, and walked out the door.

I would do my equine shopping on line from now on.

To celebrate my forthcoming birthday, I had made an appointment with a nail salon in Westport for a manicure. I was helped by two tiny Korean women. One took wonderful care of my hands, while the other gently massaged my shoulders. Would I ever find a man that was capable of understanding, and sincerely delivering, this kind of sensitivity? Had I become too hard, too crusted over, with all that I had been through in the last few years? And what had happened to my sense of humor? I could feel the confusion about my sexuality disappearing, and I realized that this ambivalence had had everything to do with Ginny bombarding me with her negative energy sucking for so many nights. As my nails dried, I resolved to have Afton help me permanently protect myself from Ginny.

That night I dreamed that I am sitting with Nick in his parked Volvo. I turn to speak to him, and discover Nick transforming into a disgusting, scaly, slimy monster, and saliva drips from his fangs. I scream in terror, and kick open the door on my side. Standing just outside is Ginny. She immediately turns into exactly the same monster.

CHAPTER ELEVEN

Lake Washington

As my birthday was a Saturday, I asked Angela to spend the day with me in Litchfield County. We loaded our kayaks on to the roof of Angela's SUV, put Abby in the back seat, and headed north on Route 7 from Ridgefield.

"That lake is going to be cold, Em," Angela complained. "Are you sure you want to do this?"

"Big chicken!" I laughed. "We have our hi-tech gear—and Abby has her PFD. It's a nice sunny day, and there's no wind. We'll be fine!"

Traffic was stop and go through Danbury and New Milford, but eased up on 202 in Washington. "Make a right here in Bridge Hollow," I told Angela, "and we can get lunch." We pulled up to the local deli and bakery, right in the center of the historic village.

"I love this place!" Angela whispered, closing the squeaky screen door, and looking around at the bead board walls, wood floors, and small white tables. "It's like something you find on vacation at the beach."

"Exactly." I said. "This whole area feels like that. My long range plan is to move up here."

"And buy a horse farm?"

"Or a lake house, and board Joy somewhere near by. Horses are everywhere in this county. Maybe both! But don't tell anyone yet, especially Denise, OK? I'm just thinking right now." I didn't mention that I had already put a postcard of Lake Washington on my life board, and the words "house on the water" underneath it.

We started on the long scenic drive around the lake to the state park. As Angela was driving this time, I was able to take in the landscape at my leisure. It was early spring, and the leaves had not yet arrived, but there were buds on the maples, and some of the dogwoods were in bloom. The water was reflecting the sky, bright blue, and the big evergreens were a beautiful contrast in deep green. It was a perfect day to kayak.

"Is this the boat that you had in New Hampshire?" Angela asked, as we carefully lowered my orange kayak from the roof.

"No, I left that one behind. I wanted to start fresh, so I took advantage of the end of season sale at Eastern Mountain Sports in Fairfield. It fits fine out the back of my Audi."

"That was quite a picture, you driving up with the red car, orange boat, and pink bandana hanging off the stern. Very colorful," Angela remarked. "And there was Abby, in her yellow PFD, her furry face barking out the window."

"I like to make a first impression that people won't forget!"

Abby trotted along with us, and jumped happily into my boat. She wagged her tail, and looked excited. I pushed Angela off, and then got in. Abby settled down in the bow, paws on the gunwales, triangular ears flapping in the slight breeze. We decided to paddle around the periphery of the lake, which I estimated would take about two hours.

As we moved past the beach, a line of about forty Canadian geese waddled down the hill, across the street, and straight into the water. Completely undisturbed by us, they glided past our boats in double file, chatting amongst themselves, and finally disappeared into the next cove.

The cattle on the opposite bank were lowing. We could see their black and white backs moving up and down in the wooded field, searching for spring grass.

"This certainly is a peaceful place," Angela remarked, as we cleared the park area.

"The energy here is serene," I replied. "I try to feel like this at the beach in Southport—I go there practically every day. It just isn't the same. And I've always been such a beach lover."

"I don't think it's the landscape, so much as the people in it, right? In Southport you are surrounded by big corporate bucks. That's going to impact the flavor of the place. In this area, there's a great deal of creativity. Artists, actors, writers. People come up here to escape the city, and feel closer to the earth. You sense that here. It's like lying in a hammock."

"This lake is loved, and the people here are serious about protecting it. Notice how there isn't one motor boat on the water right now, and this is mid morning. Not even a lonely fisherman. The silence is wonderful."

A man in a racing single appeared from the Bridge Hollow side of the lake. "Look!" Angela said. "I bet you could row here if you wanted to. Maybe launch from the park?"

"There's no dock, but sure, I can wade through weeds if I have to."

We paddled slowly along the shore. Abby stiffened as a heron landed in the cattails, searching for fish. We heard the burr-up sound of a couple of bullfrogs.

"So here we are," Angela noted. "Two women who are getting divorced. We both have our careers, and no children. We have taken the leap of faith that life with our respective husbands is no longer an option, and that something better is coming. Once the legal nonsense is finished, we are free to go where we want, and do what we want, with whoever we choose. It's a wonderful thing."

"Yes, but I'll be a lot happier when this is over, I have to be honest. I have Special Masters in less than two weeks."

"What is that, exactly? My first lawyer never explained—I just got the bill."

"Two family lawyers, supposedly experienced, are assigned by the judges to spend the day in court, getting couples to settle before trial."

"Do they do any good?"

"It depends. The court administrators usually schedule one male attorney, and one female, to promote fairness. But let's face it, these are litigators, and they tend to see every case in the same light. That is to say, 'who brought what into the marriage'."

"So this will be a waste of time?"

"Depends on who we get. There are a few good matrimonial lawyers, but for the most part, if it's people who knew Nick as a judge, or if one of the Masters is a Type A, 'if he earned it, he owns it' jerk, I can pretty much predict how the settlement conference will proceed."

"What would you prefer?"

"A pretrial with a judge, but she or he would have to be from out of the county, because again…."

"There are a lot of Nick worshipers out there."

"And just like cops, they protect their own. Especially the old boys who are hovering near retirement age."

"I guess I'm lucky that I don't have to deal with this, Em. It sounds awful."

"I feel like I'm being attacked by my own colleagues, frankly, and it's horrible. With the exception of Judge Milo, who granted my temporary alimony motion, I have almost lost faith in the Connecticut family courts. Well look," I said, suddenly brightening. "No matter what, I'll be fine. I'm a smart, healthy woman with lots of good friends, and two terrific animals. I'll get the life that I want."

Angela stopped paddling. Our kayaks bumped gently, and Abby lay down for a nap between my feet. "What kind of life do you want, Emma?"

"I don't want to practice law forever, that's for certain. And I'm not staying in Fairfield County much longer, either. Maybe I'll own an organic farm, and paint landscapes on the side. I could take in foster kids who want to learn sustainable living, or run a riding school where people learn horse care, and just have fun. I'm even doing research on goats and chickens."

"I'm speechless!" Angela said, gulping a little. "You're talking about a major life transition. Most people don't have the courage to take on something like this. I'm impressed."

"Thanks, but I feel the inevitability of the change—it's so strong, it would be nuts to stay put."

"What does Kate think about all this?" Angela asked, paddling once more.

"I haven't spoken to Kate much lately."

"Why not? She's your sounding board for everything."

"Ange, remember that summer before college? All the graduation parties were done, and we were buying stuff for our dorms and dreaming about the future? We'd hang out at Great Pond, or Sherwood Island, and talk for hours?"

"And we agreed that we'd always be friends," Angela grinned. "I remember."

"I've always wanted to be friends with my sister too, but it never quite gelled. It's as though there's a glass wall between us. We can connect only so far, and then emptiness. It makes me sad, to be honest. But I've finally accepted it."

"Listen Em," Angela began. "I've known your family since we

were kids together—you and Kate, my sister and brother—we were all going to Ridgefield High at the same time. You and I were the oldest. We had all the responsibility. Our mothers both worked, which meant that we never really had childhoods. We were little adults, and it was totally unfair."

"I agree."

"I liked your dad," Angela continued. "I knew about his drunken rages, because you told me. I thought you two were really close, although now I realize that it was an unhealthy closeness. But I never liked Audrey. She just didn't act like a mother should. She wasn't kind to me. I never felt welcome in your house."

"That makes two of us," I said drily.

"They didn't strike me as bad people; just kind of stuck. You know? Like people who live in a bomb shelter. And they wanted to keep you in the basement with them."

"And you think that Kate is one of the shelter dwellers."

"I think Kate is the next generation, yes. The few times I've seen her in town, she's so much like your mother, it's a little scary. The way she speaks to her daughter, the way she dresses, her manner in general. She's not for real, the way Audrey was never real."

"So she's playing a part?"

"I feel that she doesn't have a clue who she is, or what she wants, and she's faking her whole life." Angela paused. "And most important, I think she's always been extremely jealous of you. She never misses a chance to take a verbal shot at you."

"Kate finally admitted that to me last summer."

"Good. Maybe that's a positive sign. You're a lot smarter than she is; smarter than all of them. I think they just didn't know how to handle you. I hope it's OK that I'm saying this to you." She looked anxious.

This time I stopped paddling. We were on the Washington side of the lake, passing the beach. "Actually, I appreciate it Angela.

What you're saying fits with what I've been thinking, since Christmas."

"What happened at Christmas?"

"I blew off my family for the entire season, and Kate gave me a hard time about it. I knew that she didn't want to face Audrey alone, so she'd rather drag me in to the battle zone, knowing that with all I'm going through with the divorce, I'd be fodder for Audrey's abuse. She pulled the 'mommy' card."

"Meaning?"

"Her argument was that she has to put up with Audrey because of Hannah, and that I should be supportive of that."

"Regardless of the fact that neither Kate's daughter, nor her husband, can stand Audrey?"

"Correct. So of course it's something else. She and Tom are trying to get pregnant again. I think Kate is terrified of being as awful a mother as Audrey was, so she's over compensating."

"See? I told you. Acting a part. It's so obvious. There's a brittleness when she speaks, and her sense of humor is hard, and caustic. Even her smile is forced, and she never laughs out loud, the way you do."

"Nick actually remarked on that too, years ago. He said that Kate's eyes don't smile."

"How ironic."

"It takes one to know one, I guess." I sighed. "So I need to add loss of my only sister to my list of casualties for this year."

"Who else has bit the dust, besides Nick?"

"I think Jane has taken sides in the divorce, to Nick's benefit. She's subtle about it, but after that last dinner, I plan to keep her at arm's length from now on, at least until after the trial. The employees at my tack shop are barely able to act civilly toward me. And now Lisa."

"You said that there'd been a falling out."

"Well, I had to move Joy early, to yet another barn. I think Lisa's in the same position that I was last year. Her marriage is disintegrating, but she refuses to see it. She hasn't worked outside the home in twenty years, and she has a BA in English Literature. Her kids are getting ready to leave for college, and she's terrified of being left alone with only Jack to talk to. Now she's trying to persuade Sharon to apply to local colleges, so she won't be far from home."

"That's so sad, and so tough on the kids." Angela commented. "Families are like cesspools; really toxic. They've all been swimming around in the same shit for generations. You gotta climb out, take a shower, and jump into the river of life." She smirked.

"That's pretty profound Ange!"

"I thought so! But what happened with Lisa?"

"A bunch of things all at once. Jack decided to raise the board at Birch Creek again. The price was already too high for a farm with no indoor, and no resident trainer. I just couldn't justify the expense with the divorce pending."

"Do you think that Jack was trying to force you out?"

"Yes. Obviously he wouldn't want his wife to be friends with an experienced trial lawyer. Also, he's hit on me. Twice."

"No!"

"Oh sure. Both times in their barn, when Lisa and the kids were out."

"Did you tell her?"

"What's the point? She wouldn't believe me, and even if she did, she'd make it my fault. You know how women are."

"What about the Ginny drama? Did that create a problem?"

"That was the trigger to the blow-up. Looking back it's easy to see that Ginny calculated every button that she pushed, both to create a rift between Lisa and me, and to complicate matters with Joy. She really is one sick, twisted soul."

"So Ginny back stabbed you to Lisa? How do you know?"

"Betsy, one of the other boarders, called and told me. Ginny started with Sharon, Lisa's daughter. They'd gab during lessons, on the phone at night, and in the tack room. Then when Ginny told Lisa that she couldn't work with Sharon any more, because she felt uncomfortable about me, Lisa chose Ginny. Lisa is all about Sharon, especially Sharon's show career, and Ginny worked that angle to perfection. She's the kind of person who likes to drop bombs in the middle of the room, just to see how people react. Sharon wants to qualify for the indoor shows next fall, and she needs a trainer. So now my horse is at another barn, and Ginny drives over to Lisa's to teach Sharon, three days a week."

"What a nasty bitch!"

"Well, she's been the victim of horrific ongoing abuse, but I agree. She is at the age where she should be taking charge of her own life, and not re playing her childhood out on every nice person around her. Betrayal is what she knows."

"You're being compassionate, but that doesn't excuse Lisa's behavior."

"Like you said, families are cesspools. And Lisa is paralyzed with fear about her marriage. She just can't handle being around me, and my divorce. I had the guts to get off the merry-go-round."

"I've lost some people along the way too," Angela remarked. "I think that it's a natural part of personal growth. You evolve, but those around you who can't, or won't, drop by the wayside. It's like watching a train moving along the track. Passengers get off, others get on. But the train keeps moving."

"I had a dream like that once. A few passengers got left behind— they didn't board fast enough."

"Like Kate, and your ex friends Jane and Lisa? Not to mention poor Ginny? Yes, I bet that happens a lot."

We pulled our kayaks up on the shore of the state park beach, and re loaded them onto the car. Abby stayed in the back seat, while we used the changing facilities to get into our evening wear.

Dinner at the Warren Inn was, as always, a pleasure, and we toasted our new lives with sparkling wine, and a wonderful meal.

When we got in that night, I gave Abby her final walk of the evening, and checked my land line messages. There were three: the first two were from my sister Kate, and Denise, wishing me a lovely day. The third was Nick.

"Emma, I know it's your birthday," he said in his flat, dead-pan tone, "but I regret to inform you that Macduff went into kidney failure this week, and I had to put him down yesterday. I'll see you at the Special Masters in court on the eighteenth."

CHAPTER 12

Rowing

Our meeting with the Special Masters was scheduled for eleven am, on the third floor of the Ludlow Superior Courthouse. Don and I scanned the list at the Marshals' desk.

"Oh no!" I exclaimed. "We've got Gerald Sobel."

Don grimaced, and looked at me apologetically. "Ball game over, Em. This is going to be a complete waste of time."

It was.

Don left me in one of the conference rooms, while he went in to the meeting. He was back in less than fifteen minutes. I looked up in surprise. Don's usually buoyant face was tight with anger. He shut the door, and sat down, staring at me with an odd expression.

"Well, I knew we were in for it when Sobel came running out into the hallway to hug your soon to be ex husband."

"How very professional, and impartial of him," I remarked.

"The other Special Master was Harriet Crandall. Nice woman, good at settling cases, but no match for the Sobel/McAfee combo. McAfee played the short marriage card; he worked the disparity in your ages, the fact that you're a licensed, healthy, working attorney. He made a big noise about your horse, and how much you've spent on training and showing her over the years. You're going to love Sobel's response, Emma."

I tried to remember to breathe. "What?"

"He suggested that we shoot the horse, thereby saving time and money all around."

I didn't respond. I found that it was almost impossible to clear so much negative energy all at once. I felt suffocated.

Don pulled out a form from his briefcase. "That wasn't the worst of it Em. Take a look at this."

The document was Nick's version of the marriage as a memorandum to the Special Masters. Under "Cause of Breakdown of the Marriage" McAfee had typed in: Plaintiff wife is a lesbian.

I experienced a whirling sensation. The contents of the room whipped around me so fast, had I been standing I would have fallen over.

"What is this about Emma?" Don asked quietly. "Is there something I need to know? As it stands, Sobel has recommended two hundred and fifty thousand dollars to make this case go away. You're entitled to at least three times that. Talk to me."

I gave him a very succinct outline of the Ginny situation, including her admission that she had been a long term victim of incest, and the letter that I had subsequently received, warning me off.

"So you never had sex with this woman?"

"I never even had lunch with her, Don! How the hell did Nick find out about Ginny? I didn't meet her until after I had moved out." I suddenly froze. The answer was so obvious. Jane.

"Your friend was passing information to Nick, often when she and her husband saw him in New Hampshire. She's been pumping you for months. McAfee just told me."

I was speechless with shock.

Don got out of his chair. "I'm going to the case flow office to get a trial date. There's no point in wasting any more of your money today."

I sat there, still stunned. Betrayal from every side of me. My existence felt surreal, as though I was encased in a glass bubble. Everyone else was going along, living their normal lives. I was completely isolated. For a moment I knew exactly how Ginny felt. It was horrible.

Then practicality set in. With prep time, travel, plus the pathetic waste of a settlement meeting, this little adventure had probably cost me three thousand dollars.

Don was back. "October fifth. We agreed on two days to put on evidence. That means that the depositions will be some time in September. You can rest up till then."

Denise was thunderstruck. "Are you telling me that Jane was acting as some kind of spy for Nick? That's outrageous! It's straight out of some ridiculous mean girls movie."

"Welcome to my life, Denise. It does seem like energy vampires are everywhere, in all shapes and sizes. My big concern is that they'll subpoena Ginny to testify, or notice her deposition."

"Creepy step daddy will take care of that, though, won't he? Nick and McAfee won't get anywhere near her."

"Yes, but at what emotional cost to Ginny? She'll be open to more abuse from all of them."

Denise looked angry. "With all due respect, Emma, why on earth should you care? Look at what that bitch did to you. She messed with your head, begged you for help, and when you tried to step in, she hit you in the face with her do-not-contact whammy. Now, thanks to Jane, a tough divorce just got a whole lot more complicated. To hell with Ginny. Take care of you."

I knew that Denise was right, but I couldn't change who I was. I would always feel compassion for Ginny. People like her take a bad situation and make it worse, every time, because they're too afraid and distrustful to listen to their gut. It's a terribly sad way to go through life.

Rowing began the first week of May. My group of novices was made up of about twenty men and women over thirty-five. Under Christine's direction, we were meeting Mondays and Thursdays at 6pm for the remainder of the season, which usually ran until Halloween.

Our first day was comprised of classroom instruction in the club common room. Christine gave us a lecture on rowing vocabulary. Terms such as 'weigh enough' (stop), 'port' (left side of the boat, but rower's right, as rowers face the stern of the shell), 'starboard' (the opposite of the aforementioned), 'cant' (tilting the shell over one's head, usually to maneuver in a tight area), 'stroke' (rower in the stern; sets the pace for the rest of the crew), 'bow' (front of the boat; also the rower who steers and docks), and 'red, right, return' (general boating term meaning that red channel markers should be on one's right coming back to dock).

But if I'm rowing, should the red buoy be on my left when returning? This was very confusing.

Next, we were presented with a diagram of the river and the harbor, and shown the traffic pattern for all vessels; power or self propelled. We were to proceed in a counter clockwise fashion from the dock. Deviation was permitted only if sanctioned by a coach in a launch. We were to dock quickly, thereby making room for everyone else who was coming in, or departing. The concept was similar to air traffic controlling at an airport.

"Evenings are difficult," Christine informed us, "because the power boaters tend to be tired after work, and usually a little drunk. Also, beware of fishermen; don't get your oars tangled up in their lines. Safety on the river requires extra vigilance from all of you. When it starts to get dark earlier in the fall, we will have lights on the shells for improved visibility. Red for port, green for starboard. Any questions so far?"

Then, Christine showed us a disturbing DVD on the perils of rowing in cold water. Most of us, having seen *Titanic* at least once, were instantly terrified. I was beginning to think that jumper riding was a cream puff activity compared to this sport.

"OK!" Christine said, as soon as our teeth had stopped chattering. "Let's get you on the ergs."

We marched into the boathouse. As I had erged all winter with Christine cracking the whip, I was chosen as the demo student. Having duly pointed out all of my positional errors to the group, Christine assigned a machine to each of the rest of the class, and I got a little break.

"What do you think so far? We'll have lost at least half of these people by August," she predicted. "Another third by the end of October."

"Really? Why?"

"Rowing takes commitment. The boats are heavy to carry down and up from the dock—especially at low tide; the river gets busy in the summer, people go on vacation. It takes almost every muscle you've got to row, and a lot of people can't cut it. They bail out early, and go back to working out in the gym, and paddling a kayak on the water once in a while." She shrugged. "The Masters are out there at five in the morning, when it's usually still dark. They're serious."

And a little nuts.

"Well, you can count on me!" I said cheerily. "I've always wanted to do this, I love a challenge, and it sure beats hanging around hot, dusty horses in the middle of July."

"Good to hear!" Christine said, patting my shoulder. "We're taking out an eight on Thursday. You're going to be bow."

Forty-five minutes later we were released. I signed out a bottle of water, grabbed a towel, and moved with the rest of the lemmings toward the locker rooms.

"Muscle lady!" One of the men in my novice group, a tall, rather studly specimen with blond hair, was grinning at me. "Some of us are going up to the restaurant for dinner." I detected a slight accent. Norwegian? "Would you care to join us?"

I knew that Abby would be bursting for a walk, so I regretfully declined.

"Maybe next time," he said, with a sparkly smile. "I'll be seeing you two times a week from now until November," he reminded me. "You'll run out of excuses at some point."

Hmm. No wedding ring.

Marianne Sheehan called me at the office the next morning. I'd met her years ago at the courthouse, when she was getting a restraining order against her first husband. We'd been friends for a short time, but I hadn't heard from her in a while.

"My mother died in April, Emma."

"Oh no, I'm sorry."

"And my grandmother died in May."

I sensed a purpose to this call.

"You remember my loving siblings," she continued.

"Vaguely. I haven't seen either of them in years."

"They've hinted that there is going to be some trouble over the settling of these estates."

"Define hinted."

"At my grandmother's burial, my brother Brian walked up to our family lawyer and announced: 'Now the fun begins!'"

"I really don't know much about probate, Marianne. Isn't there someone closer to Newtown who could take care of this for you?"

"And Shannon told me that by the time they're through, I'll be living in a cardboard box."

Crikey.

Marianne started to cry. I made an appointment with her for the following day.

Denise called me from court. "I don't think I'm going to get back tonight until late, Emma. We have a situation down here."

"Our side or theirs?"

"Possibly both. The *Garraty* file. We had a real shocker in court today. I'll tell you when I see you."

Denise did not return to the office until nearly seven that night. First order of business was a double vodka martini.

"There has been some hanky-panky with Mrs. Garraty's medical reports, Em."

I gaped like a largemouth bass. "What sort of hanky-panky?"

"Changes. Deletions. Missing information. We don't even know the extent of it yet. The other side figured it out before we did."

"How?"

"Our expert's deposition. I wasn't present. George and Vicky attended the depo. Apparently, there were prior injuries that we didn't know about, so obviously we didn't disclose them. George and I were in front of Judge Rittman today. It wasn't pretty. This could mean big trouble for my old firm." She took a gulp of martini. "We're probably out of it, thank goodness. But, you never know."

"Is the judge blaming George?"

"Let's just say he wants to know what happened, when, and by whom."

Annie buzzed. "Your friend Marianne is here."

I went out to meet her. The same gorgeous smile, but definitely tired around the eyes. She handed me a file.

"There are copies of both wills. Here's the lawyer who is the executor for my mother's estate; and this is the attorney for my grandmother's estate, who is also representing my brother and sister against me regarding my mother's estate."

"He's doing both?" Not necessarily an ethics violation, but teetering on potential conflict. "Who's the executor for your grandmother's estate?"

"My sister Shannon. Did I mention that my mother had remarried seven months before she died? He's the one who found her dead in their bedroom. She had just done a new will."

"Don't tell me that your step father gets the house!"

"Just a life estate. But with my luck, he'll live another twenty years."

This case was beginning to resemble Sunday Night at the Movies. "Have the three of you discussed making the new husband an offer?"

"We can't discuss anything. Their lawyer won't talk to me, and the executor for my mother's estate never returns phone calls. There are liquid assets in both estates. I could really use an advance."

"I'll give them both a call. We'll work it out."

Angela called with big news.

"Emma! I've been talking to the powers that be here in the newsroom about your professional women's group. They'd like you and Denise to come in and be interviewed for one of the network's shows—it targets women in the state who are making a difference. You'd be aired on television, as well as the web. Are you interested?"

I skipped into Denise's office. "Want to be on TV?" I asked.

"This is amazing Emma! When do we go in?"

"Tomorrow morning. Can you do it?"

"Absolutely. What do you think the questions will be?"

"Probably along the lines of what prompted us to have the idea in the first place, what are our goals, and do we plan to expand?"

"OK. The group was your idea, and I used to be your lawyer, so I'll let you decide how much you want to divulge about your personal experience with the system."

I considered her point. "I think that I'll just keep it professional. My divorce is still pending, and I don't want to start publicly bad mouthing judges, or former judges for that matter, at least until my dissolution decree is final."

Angela met us in the lobby of the television station outside Hartford the next morning. "They want you up in the third floor studio," she said, leading us to the elevators. "Don't be nervous," she added, noting our expressions of dismay, "this will be fun. You want to get the word out there, don't you? The internet will do that, faster than anything. You'd be amazed at the number of people in the world who spend hours a day, glued to their computer screens." Angela laughed. "Way worse than we ever were with sitcoms and soap operas."

The studio took up the entire space, with just a few small offices along the walls. There were huge cameras on the floor, and suspended from the ceiling. A conversational grouping of chairs around a conference table was set up in the center of the room. A beautiful blond with an ear piece, and wearing a short, tight red dress approached us, and indicated that we should take a seat on the set.

"What, no make-up?" Denise joked.

We sat, and watched the flow of human traffic. I would never get used to seeing people walk along having conversations with invisible devices. In the old days, they would have been hospitalized for mental illness.

After about fifteen minutes, the locally famous Florence Montgomery undulated over in her tangerine suit to give us the preliminary pep talk.

"That camera will be on you," she pointed, "so please don't look directly into it. I'll be asking you questions one at a time. I'll start with you Emma, as Angela has told me that this group was your brain child. We'll be taping this interview, and later on we'll be adding your names and the CAPW web address to the bottom of the screen. We will air on Wednesday night, and the show will run on our website every night next week at eight o'clock. We will send you DVD's of the taping as well, so please be sure to leave your cards with my assistant." She paused. "Any questions?"

"How long will this segment be?" Denise asked.

"Five minutes. So please be as concise as possible, especially as there are two of you."

Florence got the signal to make her opening remarks.

She looked into another camera. "With me tonight are Westport law partners Emma Carbury and Denise Frederickson, two women who are doing an extraordinary service for Fairfield County's women. They are co-founders of the Connecticut Affiliation of Professional Women, a networking group which offers information and referrals to individuals who are facing major life transitions. Emma, what inspired you to come up with this wonderful idea?"

I breathed down into my stomach, and instantly relaxed. "For years I have represented women who have been paralyzed with fear as to how to proceed when a crisis presents itself. I wanted to provide them with a website that's a one-stop resource, free of cost to the public, to help alleviate this stress."

"Denise, I understand that you and Emma are law school classmates, as well as law partners. What would you say has kept the two of you on the same page for so long?"

"Trust," Denise answered, immediately. "Emma and I are both committed to helping people. We are aware that although lawyers tend to behave as though they are experts in such areas as mortgages, finance, and tax, in reality they rarely are. We both know when to admit ignorance, and call in a specialist."

"What categories of professional expertise are you offering on your website?" Florence asked me.

"We have women who are licensed CPAs, financial planners and advisors, and mortgage and insurance specialists. We also have career advisors, mental health professionals, and attorneys who work with trusts and estates, as well as elder law."

Florence looked at her notes. "You both do divorce work, yes? What other types of challenges are being addressed by CAPW?"

Denise answered: "Family and relationship challenges, which may include illness, special schooling needs, or criminal activity among related individuals. We also deal with retirement, aging parents, widowhood, and career changes."

"What are your goals for the group in the immediate future? Any plans to become a non profit?'

"None," Denise said firmly. "Non-profit status would generate too much paper work, which we feel would take away from the spirit of our mission."

"What is your mission?"

"We hope to dispel myths and alleviate fears, through education of our clients, and to provide quality referrals, all of which are hand picked by the two of us," Denise replied. "We carefully vet each potential addition to the network, and we meet regularly to get to know each other, and to keep each other up to date on the work that we all do."

"This is not a formal venture, correct?"

"It can't be," I responded, "because the Connecticut Bar Association will not allow lawyers and non lawyers to practice together. As Denise said, we don't want the added nuisance of filing tax returns, drafting by-laws, and obtaining the insurance coverage that would be necessary, if we were to be approved for non profit status. We like things simple and straight forward."

"Do you plan to expand into eastern Connecticut?"

"My vision, if you will, of this venture, is to expand into the rest of New England."

"We feel that every state should have a public service such as ours," Denise explained. "We don't offer pro bono work as a group; that decision is up to individual members. But we do promise to provide a comprehensive, team approach, to help solve problems."

"And the public response has been positive?"

Denise grinned. "So far! From men, as well as women. Most of our clients express wonder that something like our group hasn't materialized before now."

Florence looked interested. "Why do you suppose that is?"

"It's all about control," I answered, with feeling. "If a woman feels supported and buoyed up by a positive network behind her, she is frankly not going to be easy prey for controlling predators. It is when people are alone, and terrified," I concluded, "that the blood suckers can move in."

CHAPTER 13

Erik

After several weeks of rowing up and down the river in a quad, Samantha and I asked permission to take out a recreational double.

Unlike horses, rowing shells do not walk on their own. Doubles are at least thirty feet in length, and the heavier recreational boats weigh over eighty pounds. Juggling such a beast between two women was a challenge. We collected our oars first, and carried them down to the dock.

"Oh no," Sam groaned. "Low tide. Look at the grade of the gangplank! Getting back up to the boathouse is going to be a real bitch."

We searched among the racks until we found our target vessel. Sam made the call: we lifted the shell, canted it carefully so that the riggers did not get snagged on other boats, and eased the double on our shoulders into the ninety degree turn just before the gangplank.

Suddenly, I felt the stern lift out of my hands. Erik had come up behind me, and taken the weight off my shoulder.

"Here you go, ladies," he said, in his lovely soft Swedish accent. "I've got it. Emma, you can go help Sam with the bow."

The three of us put our toes over the edge of the dock, flipped the shell, and carefully lowered it into the water. "See you out on the water!" Erik said, and sprinted back up to the boathouse.

Sam smirked. "That guy is all over you!" She said. "Makes me wish that I wasn't happily married. All this attention is very flattering, don't you think?"

After several weeks in the rowing program, we had learned that Erik was a doctor—a gyn/ob, with a busy practice in Norwalk. Originally from Sweden, he had lived in the U.S. since medical school. He had just turned fifty, was about six feet tall, and still had thick blond hair to go with his green eyes.

"I wish he'd stop hovering and make his move," Sam said. "How hard is it to want to meet for a drink?"

"Maybe he's heard that I'm getting a divorce," I replied, practically. "That's something that I'd shy away from, to be honest. No one needs all that extra drama in their lives."

We screwed our oars in to the locks, and got into our double. As bow, I steered us across the river so that we were heading up stream, then Samantha, as stroke, set the pace. Sam and I were perfectly matched as rowing partners. We moved along the river in a steady cadence, completely synchronized.

We were out for an hour and twenty minutes. Christine motored back and forth among the boats in her coach's launch, made suggestions, and occasionally set us some drills. We watched swans drifting elegantly by the shore, looking for dinner. Several kayakers paddled by, and one fisherman considerately waited for us to pass before he cast his line.

By 7:30 we had pulled our shell out of the brackish water, and were hosing it down on saw horses on the dock. There remained the daunting ascent back to the club; the tide was even lower at this point in the evening, and the gangplank was pitched at an alarmingly steep angle.

Then Erik pulled up in his quad with three other men. Leaving them to fend for themselves, he attached himself to the bow of our double. Sam and I both thanked him with feeling, and in no time we had our shell secure on its rack, and were walking back down to get our oars.

Erik was just bringing up the stern of his quad. "Joining us for dinner upstairs, ladies?" He asked. "There's about eight of us so far."

I looked at Samantha. "See you in fifteen," she announced, grinning at me. "I just have to check with my babysitter."

The Rowing Club restaurant was lit with nautical lanterns and candles. The sun was fading as Sam and I took our seats at the long table that had been set up for us on the balcony, overlooking the river. Christine had organized appetizers for the table, and she passed the plates of fried shrimp and potato skins as Sam ordered a chardonnay for me, and a club soda with lime for herself. "Still nursing!" She announced.

"Aha!" Erik replied. "How long has it been?"

"Five months, but this is my second. We seem to be holding our own in the milk department."

"Who was your doctor?" Erik asked, with professional curiosity.

"Didn't have one," Sam said, grabbing an onion ring. "Don't believe in them. Jake and I went with a midwife, and I delivered both our boys at home."

Rebecca whistled. "That was brave of you!"

"Why?" Sam demanded. "Hospitals are terrible places. Germs everywhere, and the horrible energy of people sick and injured, or dead. Relatives flipping out. Nurses bothering patients at all hours of the night, so they never get any rest. And doctors playing god in their white coats and their detached 'I'm already late for my tee off' attitudes."

"We're not all like that," Jason replied, waving his martini. "Some of us are committed to patient care."

"You're the gastro guy, right?" Sam scoffed. "Didn't I hear you just last week laughing about poking some 'middle aged broad' up the butt with your colon scope, or whatever. Now there's an example of medical compassion!"

Jason's face turned red, and he did not respond.

Rebecca said: "I'm a doctor's wife, and I'm a non practicing RN, so I have mixed emotions on this topic."

Julie took a gulp of her beer. "I'm with Sam on this one, people. I had a ghastly time with two ENTs last year. I went in with a mild case of buzzing in my ear. They did everything imaginable to me, including two MRIs—terrifying me with talk of brain tumors. Turns out that I had had a bad case of flu, and some minor nerve damage. You wouldn't believe the pills those two fools had me on. Steroids, muscle relaxers, antibiotics. Finally, I went to a naturopath, who figured out the problem." She took a deep breath, clearing the experience. "Beats me why anyone would listen to a doctor. I'm never going to waste my time with an MD again."

Christine looked interested. "Who's your ND? I go to a guy in Fairfield for my Lyme Disease. He's phenomenal. I'm totally hooked on homeopathy."

Jason rolled his eyes. "I can't believe you gals! Next you'll be telling us that you beat tom-toms and mash herbs and dance by the full moon!"

"That's Emma's gig," Sam replied. "She's into the Shaman deal. Looks like pretty soon you quacks are going to be out of a job."

Erik smiled politely. "There are still plenty of babies being born in the hospital, Samantha."

"You gynecologists are the worst!" Julie suddenly looked ferocious. "Your entire practice is based on creating fear in women, so that they come back often, and do whatever you say, humiliation and expense be damned. It's a disgrace. I have at least five friends who have gone through horrific scares with breast exams and so-called abnormal Pap smears, for no reason." She got up, shaking with rage. "I'd like to see one of you smug shits get a needle stuck into your dick, or have your balls squashed over and over by a metal plate. Nothing like a little terror, is there boys?"

Julie left the restaurant very quickly.

"My goodness!" Sam said, after a pause. "I don't think I could have put that better myself."

"Me either," I agreed. "I always tell clients: the worst thing a lawyer can do is take your money. Now think about what doctors do to people, every day."

Sam signaled the waitress for another club soda. "Yep, like I said. Your days are numbered."

Jason slammed his Scotch and soda down on the table. The waitress retrieved his glass and scurried away.

"So!" Christine said, ever the teacher. "We've been really lucky with the weather so far. Is everyone enjoying rowing?"

Erik ran up as I was getting into my Audi. "Interesting evening, wouldn't you say?" He asked, leaning against the door. "I'm sorry that we didn't get a chance to talk."

"Very illuminating," I replied, keeping it cool. "I admit that I do get tired of hearing clients tell me that they're on medication—it's always something."

"Well," Erik said, softly. "You looked great tonight, really. I'd like to see more of you."

I laughed. "You'll see me on Saturday morning. Our group has hired Christine for an extra coaching, remember?"

He squeezed my arm, and suddenly leaned over and kissed me on the cheek.

"Saturday then. I'm looking forward to it."

On Friday evening my landlord had invited me over to his house for cocktails, to discuss a new lease. I had not wished to be locked into a full year contract when I first moved in, so we had agreed on six month increments.

Fred Crowley was an elderly man, at least eighty years of age. He lived in a big white house on the water in Southport, and his back porch had a gorgeous view of the harbor and the yacht club. A former political advisor to President Reagan, Fred had rounded out his career by teaching at Yale, and guest lecturing in the United States and Europe. He had written several books on American Foreign Policy, one of which had been required reading when I was studying political science at Vanderbilt. A recent widower, his three daughters all lived within half an hour of him. Fred was an interesting man, and I enjoyed talking to him.

He poured me a glass of chardonnay.

"How's your divorce going, Emma?" He indicated that I should help myself to the cheese and crackers.

I took a piece of cheddar. "Slowly. My husband is doing his best to grind me down."

"But you won't let him get away with that!" Fred chuckled. "You strike me as a very tough young lady."

I sighed. "Tough, but tired."

"What do you think you want to do when you're done? Will you buy in Southport?"

"I don't plan to stay in the area, frankly. I'd like my own horse farm, which requires lots of land. Fairfield County is not terribly accommodating in that respect."

"No," he agreed. "Not much raw real estate left, and what there is, costs too much."

"I've loved living so close to the Sound," I admitted, "but I'm really looking forward to the kind of privacy that a big piece of property can provide."

"The neighbors aren't bothering you, are they?" Fred inquired. "I've heard nothing but good things about you, and your dog. She's a neighborhood favorite, apparently."

"Abby certainly knows how to work a crowd."

The topic turned to the President's recent trip to the Middle East. Finally, Fred brought out the old lease.

"Can you do your lawyer thing, and just extend the current terms for another six months?" He asked. "It would be so much simpler."

I hand wrote our agreement at the bottom of the document. We both signed, and Fred left the room to make a copy for me.

I stood up. "Thank you so much for an interesting evening, Fred. I would never have been able to have a discussion like this with my husband. He would have pontificated, while I tuned out, with the occasional nod and smile. I enjoy talking to you; you are an extremely intelligent man."

That's when it happened. I was about to reach for my bag, when Fred, moving faster than I would have thought possible for a man his age, suddenly had both hands wrapped hard around my rib cage. He slobbered me on the cheek twice. His fingers were positioned right under my breasts.

Although Fred was taller, I'm sure I could have knocked him down with one arm.

However, this was the man who owned my home, and I did not want to have to look for a new one in the near future, especially in the midst of a protracted divorce. I felt like a serf in the Middle Ages, and the French term *les droits de seigneur* flashed through my mind. The rights of the lord of the manor. The law of the landlord. Domination and intimidation. Fred felt that he was entitled to behave this way toward me, because he controlled where I lived.

I grabbed my purse, shoved my copy of the lease in the back pocket, and ran out of the house, without another word.

Several hours later, I was still fuming. That appalling old man. I wondered how often he had cheated on his wife before she died.

The alarm rang at five a.m. on Saturday morning. I looked at the clock in dismay, and then dragged myself out of bed. Abby declined to join me. I had allotted myself half an hour toward personal beautification in preparation for the morning group row, knowing that Erik would be there. I turned the taps on in the shower, and waited for the hot water to come on. Minutes later, I was still waiting. The water was ice cold.

As I washed my hair, shivering and screaming profanities, I suddenly realized that under normal circumstances I would have called Fred for a problem with the boiler. Screw it, I said out loud. I'll pay for the damn plumber myself.

My rowing class had agreed to meet in the common room for breakfast at 6 a.m. Sam and I were among the first to arrive, so we ordered egg and cheese sandwiches, and put our water bottles down at a table by the French doors.

"Has he asked you out yet?" Sam whispered, watching Erik come through the door with his usual band of male medical cronies.

"Nope!" I finished my chai latte. "I was hoping that today would be the day. It's the weekend, we're not all exhausted from a long day of work, and he's been flirting with me for what seems like ages now."

"He certainly seems to have singled you out, Em," Sam agreed.

Rebecca stopped by our table. "Mind if I sit, ladies?" She put down her doughnut and coffee, and looked at her watch. "Christine should be here pretty soon. We need to be getting out on the water."

"We were just laughing about Doctor Flirtatious over there," Sam said. "If I had known that obstetricians looked that good, I would have had my kids in the hospital after all."

"You mean Erik? Yeah," Rebecca replied. Then she dropped the bomb. "His poor wife. That guy is *way* too fond of women."

I sat stunned. Talk about a cold shower.

"His wife? Erik is married?" Sam was indignant. "He sure doesn't act like it."

"Married with three kids," Rebecca informed us, breezily. "Jenna is a tiny little thing, very quiet. We see her a lot at medical functions—they never talk to each other. Erik's too busy working the room. My husband is a pediatrician," she added.

So Erik had counted on the fact that the men in our group would not give him away. He had reckoned without the women.

Christine arrived, and we were assigned to our shells. Sam and I got a light weight racing double, only sixty pounds, and easily carried it down to the dock. The tide was in, mercifully, so the grade down to the water was negligible. We had secured our oars in the riggers, and were stepping into the boat, when Erik and three of the other men came down with a quad, and put it in the water behind us. Erik sidled up to me and bumped me with his forearm.

"You look wonderful in the morning, sweetheart," he breathed in my ear, his Swedish accent no longer even remotely attractive.

"Thanks," I retorted. "I'll be sure to tell your wife that you think so."

Erik stepped back with alarm, his countenance an unappealing vermilion.

Snorting with glee, Samantha and I pulled away from the dock.

I caught a glimpse of Erik's face as we crossed the river channel and headed upstream. He was clearly furious.

I called five plumbers until I finally found one that could come out to a job on a Saturday afternoon. He pulled into my driveway in a white pickup at three o'clock. The man was about sixty, with a bull dog face, and nearly as wide as he was tall. Abby sniffed him suspiciously, and I took him down to the cellar to address my lack of hot water.

"Looks pretty simple," he announced. "I can fix this in about fifteen minutes."

I sighed with relief.

"How long have you owned this place?" The plumber asked.

I decided to be friendly. I really wanted a good shower.

"Oh I don't own it."

"How long are you here for?"

"Don't know yet. There are lots of variables."

"Huh? Anyone else live here with you?"

I stiffened. "Why do you ask?"

"I just noticed that your kitchen table is set up for one, that's all. No harm in my question, is there?" He turned and leered at me.

"I'll be in the living room with the checkbook when you're ready to leave," I replied shortly. Abby followed me up the stairs.

CHAPTER 14

Scissors

"Remember that like attracts like," Afton explained, at our next session. "This explains such sayings as 'what goes around, comes around,' 'misery loves company,' and 'be careful what you ask for.' What you send out, you will receive. It's the law of the Universe."

"So how does that explain all the jerks that I've been dealing with lately?" I asked, somewhat bitter. "My landlord, the dirty old man. That creepy plumber. The charming crotch doctor at the club. Not to mention Ginny, and my dear energy slurping husband. Are you saying that I was asking for these people? Am I one of them?" I demanded, horrified.

Afton laughed. "No, of course you're not one of them! But wounds attract wounds. That's the simple answer to the Ginny question. Think, Emma. You were a victim of a form of incest as a child. Incest that involved your father. Your soon to be ex husband was also sexually abusive to you, and he used money, and verbal assaults, to control you. I know that you've worked on these issues in Reiki, but you're still under attack in your divorce, and you're energetically vulnerable. Moreover, you feel betrayed, and to a certain degree devalued, by your own profession, which is comprised of what you call the 'old fart brigade'—men and women who are seemingly supporting your husband against you. These feelings send out a lower vibration."

"So what happened?" Afton continued. "Ginny tuned in to that frequency. So did all of those men who you just mentioned. They sensed a frailty in your luminous field, and they charged right in. The key here is to raise your frequency, so high that these people can't even see you, much less weaken you. Does that make sense?"

"But what about the lesbian thing?" I asked, still confused.

"What do you really feel, if you drop down into your gut, and tune out your mind? Are you a lesbian?"

I was silent for a moment. I slowed my breathing, and just allowed myself to be.

"No." I said firmly. "I'm not. For a while there, I was practically convinced that I was going to start driving without a stick. Then I met Erik. He was totally unavailable—and I feel sorry for his wife, that poor woman—but on the plus side, he certainly got my juices flowing. I began to feel more like myself again, only better."

"Why better?"

"Because it was easy to just tip my hat at him, say thanks but no thanks, and walk away. In the old days, I would have considered his feelings and needs, rather than my own. I probably would have blamed his wife! Now, I can't tolerate even a moment of drama."

Afton nodded. "Drama is for people who need to feed off other people's energy. A truly whole, self satisfied person will always run in the opposite direction. Emotionally healthy individuals tend to prefer comedy, in fact. Laughing, like happiness, occurs on a high vibration. That's assuming that the laughter isn't at someone else's expense."

"Oh! You've just explained why I don't bother to watch TV anymore. In fact, I've canceled my cable service. I watch DVD's; movies, mostly, or old sitcoms that I used to love. I can't stand violence, especially if it's happening to children, or animals."

"It's all about vibration. You're on a much higher frequency now. This means no more rescue and sacrifice. No more saving people who aren't ready to be saved. Soon you won't be able to eat meat, either."

I was amazed. "Already there! I'm down to poultry, fish and seafood. Lots of eggs, and beans. I'm always trying new recipes, and I'm taking cooking classes, so I don't get bored."

"You see? But back to your feelings. You're going to need a relationship that matches your new high vibration. That means a very special kind of man. Oh yes, they exist," Afton said quickly, reading my dismay. "I've got one myself. It will happen. But first, let's unhook the others, and get you strong. You have to be absolutely clear on your intention, or the Ginny dreams will continue. Do you want them to stop?"

"Absolutely."

"Then let's begin."

"So what did she do?" Angela asked, agog. "Because I would sure like her to work her voodoo for me!"

"It started out like my other healing sessions. She had me bring up my feelings of disgust about all the people in my life who don't understand boundaries. She banged her drum and shook her rattle. She burned sage. What was different this time was that I heard the noise of scissors."

"Scissors?"

"Afton explained that she was cutting the energetic cords that attached me to people like Ginny. She said that Nick still had a hook in me too, but she got rid of all of them."

"Where are these cords attached to you? This is a little creepy."

"It *is* a little weird, you're right. One was on my liver, the rest in my solar plexus, the belly button area. It's one of the chakras. They're energy centers—each has its own vibration, and color. The higher up the body, the higher the vibration."

"Wow," Angela said. "I need to do some reading. But do you feel better? Are you invisible to low-lifes now?"

"Supposedly! I feel lighter anyway. Time will tell. I'll see Erik at rowing on Thursday. If he walks by without even noticing me in my tight Lycra outfit, I'll know that Afton's hocus pocus worked."

CHAPTER 15

Mutants

The June meeting of the Book Club met in our conference room, and Eliot had ordered food from a caterer down the street. I got out the big blender, and made margaritas for everyone. We were discussing *Mutant Message Down Under* by Marlo Morgan.

Dottie helped me by slicing limes. "I was sorry to hear about Jane," she said. "I wondered why she didn't show for the May discussion."

"I wasn't sure if I had all the facts then—and I was too devastated to talk about it."

Dottie ran a slice of lime around the rim of five glasses, and dipped them into the salt dish. "Did you wonder if I had been the one who spilled the beans?"

"Because you work for Nick's firm? Honestly, no. You're an open minded person, Dorothy, and frankly, I didn't feel as though you had an ax to grind in my direction."

"But you knew that Jane did?"

"She's in her early sixties, contemplating retirement. Her kids are grown. Her husband Pete was hatched from the same white male supremacy nest as Nick—men are superior, women are subordinate. She told me herself that she was raised to believe that if a couple fights, the marriage is over. Forty years is a long time to keep your mouth shut. Pete's family is originally from Italy, on both sides, so he's a vocal guy."

"And she's Irish Catholic. Now *there's* a church that teaches obedience and suffering at the graduate level."

"Exactly. Consider my scenario: I'm a lawyer. I didn't spend twenty years of my life raising children and supporting my husband's career, and when I knew that I was miserable in my marriage, I got out. Bottom line? I didn't follow the script." I poured out frozen margaritas for Angela, Eliot, Denise, Dottie, and myself. "For a few months I wondered whether or not I might be a lesbian. I guess that was the last straw for Jane. Too much freedom of thinking for her to handle. The saying goes that 'a woman knows what a woman wants.' Bet you anything that Pete doesn't have a clue what Jane wants in bed, and Jane would never volunteer."

"So she sold you down the river to your husband."

"That's what my lawyer heard from his lawyer. Funny, I remember just a year ago, when we were discussing *Gaudy Night* at my house—Jane complemented me on my ability to stick to my gut and stay detached from the crowd."

"You're being magnanimous. She should have taken a page from your book."

"Most people don't. That's the whole point of the discussion tonight."

Denise opened the meeting with a short plot summary.

"This is a work of fiction based on a true story. The heroine is a doctor from the Midwest who specializes in acupuncture. She moves to Australia at the age of fifty to conduct a five year project, integrating traditional medical practices with preventative natural health education. She is invited to what she thinks is going to be an awards ceremony, given by an Aboriginal tribe. Instead, she is conducted on a three month walkabout across the continent. This story, her message, is the relaying of the spiritual ideals of an ancient people to the world."

Angela, as a journalist, was a natural successor to Jane as group leader.

"Why do the Real People refer to the author as a Mutant?"

"I made a note of the definition," Dottie said, flipping to the end of the book. "*Mutant* appears to be a state of mind, and has nothing to do with race. The term describes someone who has shut out the ancient ways and universal truths. According to this story, there are a lot of Mutants out there."

"All right," Angela grinned. "Then what is Oneness?"

"Mutants believe that everyone is separate," I replied, recalling what my research had taught me: shamanic practices are world wide. "But we are all one. The Real People explain that while Mutants have different beliefs, and one's religion is not another's, the Real People know that all life is one life, and truth is the same for everyone. They teach that all of our actions help, or hurt, everyone. While Mutants think of themselves, and separateness, the Real People are concerned with all of us—past, present, and future."

Dottie wanted to talk about telepathy. "Do we believe in it, this mind-speak? The author wonders about the silence of her companions, until she realizes that they are always talking to each other, even across great distances. They tell her that this is the way people are meant to communicate."

"It means being completely honest, and having nothing to hide," Denise said. "We must have unconditional acceptance of ourselves, and others. So, is it possible?"

"Oh, it's possible," I replied, thinking of Ginny. "Even in Dreamtime."

"That brings us to healing," Angela said. "One of the tribe suffers a compound fracture of his leg, just to show the author how their medicine works. The next day he is up and around, completely whole. The author, as a doctor, is flabbergasted by this miracle. She concludes that no doctor, at any place or time, has ever been a healer. A person's healing comes from within. The author wonders if Western illness is nothing more than a reaction to mental programming. The Real People explain to her that illness is the body's way of communicating with us. Slowing ourselves down forces us to assess those areas of our lives that require mending. Relationships, fear, beliefs, lack of forgiveness, and so forth. The author writes that Western culture is based on a core of fear, and that it is making us sick."

Eliot said: "I didn't really get this book. These people hijack the woman, burn her clothes, her ID, even her jewelry! And then they march her off into the outback wearing a wraparound rag, and no shoes. She eats bugs and reptiles, is buried in the earth, swims in a crocodile pond, suffers from thirst and heat, and then moves back to the U.S., convinced that this tribe of Aboriginals, who live off the grid, have got it right. What a god awful existence!"

No one seemed shocked at this speech. Perhaps we were each thinking the same thing: I would have pulled my gold watch out of the fire, and run screaming for the first policeman, instead of walking in the wild for months, as this author did.

"I think the point is that we as a culture have forgotten to live in community." Denise said. "We roll our eyes at the Amish, who refuse to use modern conveniences, but perhaps they know more than we realize."

"The concept of collective consciousness is foreign to most of us in the Western world," agreed Angela. "What is beingness?"

"I think it's about living in the moment, and being grateful," I began, wishing that I truly felt that I could do either for any length of time.

"I got that beingness was releasing attachment to things, and beliefs. The Real People explain that this is a world of abundance. They prove that whatever they need is provided, when they ask, and in return, they are always grateful to the Universe," Denise said. "Think about when it is the author's turn to be leader of the group. They desperately need water, but the tribe refuses to help her find it. When she finally remembers to *be* water, it appears, very quickly. This was her test. The People explain that all tests are repeated, in various forms, until we pass. She refers to this lesson as a right-brain, left-brain conflict, but I feel that it's more than that. I think this is all about surrender. If we release what we've been taught by parents, teachers, religions, and government—the Universe will manifest what we need."

"But what about what we want?" Eliot demanded. "I don't need a BMW, but boy do I enjoy driving one! Is this bad? Why can't we have comforts and conveniences?"

"Spirituality, in my opinion, has nothing to do with poverty," Angela replied. "It has to do with attitude. Abundance means that there is plenty for everyone on this planet. It is the illusion of separateness, and scarcity, and the compulsion to grab, grab, grab that keeps people living in slums and fighting wars. This book is teaching us that all of that is unnecessary."

"And detrimental to the planet," Denise added. "The author says that the pivotal part of the journey for her was the night they spent in the sacred cave, location carefully undisclosed. There the Real People reveal to her that they are having no more children, and are leaving Planet Earth. They are the direct descendents of the first beings, they explain, and that it is their group consciousness that has held the earth together. They tell her that the people on this planet have been so destructive that we have given part of the soul of the land away. The author has been chosen to teach the Western world that it is imperative to revere nature; the land, the plants and the animals. They are here to balance the planet, and to teach us as companions, and by example. We must reverse the terrible damage that has been done, before we destroy the planet. The Real People can no longer help us."

"This sounds serious," Eliot said, frowning.

"Yes," I said. "Everything is changing. Can't you feel it? The weather has been crazy the last few years. There's an intensity that's new, and time is moving quicker than it ever has. This is everybody's problem."

Dottie looked at her notes. "We can assist the healing by changing how we feel. This is what the tribe teaches the author. It is all about intent, which is manifested by action. Apparently we have been given this planet, and the gift of free will, as a kind of school for the use of our emotions. Look at how the Real People treat each other. They don't play games in which someone has to lose. They are never competitive. They work together, each bringing his or her own talents to the community. They share, they keep each other fed and healthy and warm. They observe, but they do not judge."

"The tribe understands that nothing that happens is by chance," I concluded. "They have faith in the divine plan. So, no fear. They know that all spirits are forever, and once you get that, really, what is there to be afraid of?"

"How's the rowing going, Emma?" Angela asked, as we gathered up our belongings. We watched as several club members moved smoothly down the river, a coach in a launch in their wake. "I'm impressed that you've taken up such a tough sport in your forties."

"We started on the river in early May, learning in recreational boats, but Christine has a few of us in racing shells already. It's like sitting on a big pencil, and a little unsettling at times—the river isn't all that clean, and I'd rather not flip over. But I'm loving it!

There's something exhilarating about moving so quickly and quietly through the water, and you can't beat the exercise! My chiropractor says that my back is solid muscle. I've signed up for a long weekend of rowing camp in New Hampshire at the end of this month. I wanted to wait until the lake was warmer up there."

"Have you met any men at your club?" Eliot asked.

"Sure. They're all married." I grinned.

Dottie stayed behind when Eliot and Angela went out to the parking lot.

"Emma and Denise, there's something that I'd like you to think about, if you would please. I've decided to leave my firm, effective at the end of June, and drop down to freelance part time hours. Let me know if I can be any help to you. I've got experience in civil, family, and real estate. I can do title searches, and I'm a notary."

Denise brightened. "I could sure use your help with my civil jury files. Thanks Dot. I'll be emailing you soon."

Afton emailed me her jpeg and career bio, as well as an article that explained the basics of her Shamanic Practice, focusing specifically on Soul Retrieval. I forwarded the information to the group web designer, who posted it on our site. Afton was now a member of the Connecticut Affiliation of Professional Women. I felt that it was time that her work was mainstreamed.

CHAPTER 16

Rowing Camp

Rowing camp was scheduled for the last four days in June. On Thursday morning I packed my water gear, dropped Abby off at the vet's for boarding, and pointed the Audi north on the very familiar drive up I-91 in Vermont, to New Hampshire.

From the time that Nick and I had begun dating, nearly fourteen years before, I had been making this trip to his second home on Pequot Lake, on the western side of the state. The house had always been a place of renewal for me. Wrap around decks on two of the three levels looked out on the water. The property was situated on a peninsula, and sparkling blue, outlined by the deep green of the surrounding pines, was the view from every point in the house. One of the reasons I had stalled so long before leaving the marriage was my love for the lake, and the easy lifestyle that came with it. We ate many of our meals outside, slept with the French windows wide open all summer, biked to the store for groceries, and the dogs were blissfully happy taking long walks, and kayak rides with us.

Extreme unhappiness can be tolerated for just so long. I found that I was either going to get out, or drink myself into a self medi-cated cocoon, as my father had done. I chose the healthy route. There are other lakes, I reasoned, and I began fine tuning the dream of a waterfront property of my own.

I passed the exit for Pequot Lake and traveled another twenty miles north. The backdrop of mountains and dairy farms in Vermont was breathtaking, as always. I crossed the Connecticut River into New Hampshire at exit fifteen. Signs for Linlithgow Hall pointed east, eight more miles.

The exclusive boarding school, founded by a wealthy titled Scot in the early nineteenth century, was situated on a campus which included about twenty stone buildings in a distinctly British style of architecture, hundreds of acres of grass lawns and old for-ests, as well as Copper Lake. I checked in at the alumni office, and was assigned a room in Kirkwood, on the second floor. The floors were of old oak, the walls of thick plaster, and huge case-ment windows opened out onto views of the water. The furniture, two single beds, two dressers, and two desks with built in book shelves, were all of dark walnut, and in surprisingly good condi-tion. There was a fireplace, stocked with wood, in the middle of the far wall, and a couple of throw rugs in colorful tartans. In lieu of a closet, a huge old cherry wardrobe with mirror stood in one corner. This room had to be quite a chilly place in the winter.

I unpacked my bags, noted the location of the nearest commu-nity bathroom, and proceeded down the path to the boathouse. Located on the southern curve of Copper Lake, which was shaped like a teardrop, the pointed end at the north, the boathouse was a modern white clapboard structure, trimmed in the school colors of royal blue and gold. Racks of eights, fours, and quads lined the driveway, and peering inside, I found a young man in black Lycra with a clipboard, assigning singles and oars to campers who had already checked in.

"Welcome to our adult sculling program," he smiled. "May I have your name?"

I gave it to him. He had all my information, including my height and weight, the fact that I was a novice recreational rower, and that I was a member of the club in Westport.

"I have you down for number five," he pointed to a blue boat on the rack along the wall, "and the number ten oars. Have you ever rowed in a racing shell before?"

"Yes," I replied. "But not in a single. Just doubles."

"Well, this is the place to learn!" He grinned. "I'm Fred. I'm the assistant coach for the varsity girls team here."

"Aha," I replied, noting his big blue eyes, cropped red hair, and his six foot muscular frame, already perfectly tanned. "I'll bet you're very popular."

"We came in second in the division this year," he replied, missing the point. "Orientation begins in an hour, here in the boathouse. Please be dressed to row." He turned to the fifty-something woman standing to his right.

I strolled to the school store and amused myself by buying postcards, and a royal blue fleece blanket with the school logo embroidered in gold on one corner. Abby would love it.

The sun was warm, but there was a good breeze. Having clad myself in navy Lycra and Teva water sandals, I grabbed my Westport Rowing Club jacket in shocking, high visibility pink, and my water bottle, and arrived back at the boathouse in plenty of time for the meet and greet section of the weekend.

I have never done well in groups. Nick had often complained that as I was such a loner, I should live in a cave, and have supplies delivered. He really didn't understand, but that was hardly surprising. People tend to talk about themselves. It was rare to meet a good listener, and even more unusual to find someone who enjoyed true conversation—the give and take of people engaged in a dispassionate discussion of ideas. In my experience, most preferred to yammer at each other at rapid fire speed, thus avoiding interruption.

There was about thirty of us in the program. I noted three men, and two high school aged girls. The remainder was comprised of middle aged women. Except for the aforementioned girls, I was probably the youngest person in the group.

All but one of the coaches lined up at the front of the room were men. My new buddy Fred was tucked away at one end; the female at the other. At the center was a tall, thin, dark haired man in his early thirties. He called us to attention.

"I'm Trevor Mullen, the Head Rowing Coach here at Linlithgow Hall. To my left are Philip, my assistant coach, and Bridget, who coaches the girls." Bridget gave us a quick smile. "To my right are Jim, who manages the boathouse and the docks, and Fred, who is Bridget's assistant." Jim did not acknowledge the introduction, but Fred waved to his new fans. "OK then. We will go around the room, and have each of you tell us your name, and rowing experience."

I always tuned out at these things. Odds were that I would never see another person in this room after Sunday afternoon. Why pretend to care who they were?

My turn came about a third of the way through the assembly.

I used my courtroom voice. "I'm Emma Carbury. I live in Fairfield, Connecticut, and I'm a member of the Westport Rowing Club." That woke up Trevor. WRC is an Olympic level training facility, and about as high end as it got on the East Coast. "I just started erging and rowing this season, and I've never flipped a boat, so I'm particularly interested in learning to recover from an accidental immersion."

There was some laughter, and then to my dismay, everyone after me proceeded to include the number of times he or she rolled their boats in their intros.

The talking stick finally got back to Trevor. With a smirk aimed right at me, "Now that we've heard everybody's flipping history, let's get on with orientation. Basic rules: never carry your boat without a partner; carry your oars blades first; when taking the boat in, or out of the water, observe that the skeg on the bottom of the boat does not hit the dock. DO NOT set the boat on the dock. Traffic MUST move counter clockwise around the perimeter of the lake. Boats go back into the boathouse stern first. Finally, hose off your boat after each row." He paused his dissertation. "The water temperature is currently a refreshing sixty-five degrees. We will start the program with Jim giving a demonstration of backing and turning. Then we'll have each of you experience the dreaded flip recovery." He smirked again. "We have college students here as interns to help you with your boats. Feel free to make use of them."

Jim was already sitting in a bright orange single by the dock. "Right," he said, obviously a Brit. "This boat is a Kronholm; probably the best shell on the market today." I sighed, thinking of how many times over the years I had heard a horseperson refer to a specific saddle as the best on the market. The pronouncement changed, predictably, every two to three years.

"I'll start by stating the obvious," Jim continued in his baritone Queen's English. "When we row, we are facing the stern, in the opposite direction from the one in which we are traveling. When we 'back,' we are literally backing the boat up, just as you would if you put your car in reverse. I will demonstrate." He squared the blades, and pushed the oars away from him. The single moved toward the dock. "The key here," he said, "is to make the quarter turn, toward your feet, to bring the oars back to you. Do not try to feather your blades. This will defeat the forward progress." The man was amazing. He moved that twenty-six foot long shell as though he was merely walking on the water.

The river turn was next. I was dazzled. Jim's orange Kronholm did an about face on a dime. The fancy oar work was beyond me, but I was determined to understand it by the end of the weekend.

"Right," he said again. "Time for the flipping." The boat went over, and within seconds, Jim was back in place, looking at us expectantly. "Everyone clear? Excellent. Philip will take over from here."

Philip was about sixty-five. His bio in the handout said that he was a retired university coach, who also taught American history. He had a kind, almost grandfatherly way about him. I felt immediately at ease, and when he asked for a volunteer, I raised my hand. Get it over with fast, is my motto.

Funny that something we were all so worried about happened very quickly, and without incident. In I went into the brisk spring lake water. I grabbed the ends of both oars with my left hand, the opposite gunwale with my right, and I leapt across the boat, repositioning my rear on the rolling seat. I stuck my feet back on the sliders, and grinned, waiting for applause. It came. I hoisted myself back on to the dock, considerably moistened, and the next contestant was up. Frankly, a wet exit from a kayak is a lot tougher, especially if one is wearing a spray skirt.

Once each of us had been dipped, Trevor returned to announce that we should get our boats and start our first row, which, he revealed, would be recorded. "We'll have lunch in MacPherson

Dining Hall, and then review the videos on the second floor of the boathouse. Oars, everyone!"

Postcard to my sister Kate, a picture of the Linlithgow Hall campus, haloed in spring green on the front:

My god Kate! I feel like I've been drafted, and this is Boat Camp. We rowed twice today, total of three hours on the water, and got reviewed via the floating camera crew. I was told that my oars need to drop into the water faster, and that confidence in my drive needs to be a lot stronger (!) When we aren't forced to row, we're forced to stretch, and then we eat. Food's good, though. I'm going to need heavy calories to get through this weekend. Gorgeous weather so far.

Love, Emma

Postcard to my law partner Denise, a picture of the boathouse swathed in mist on the front, one lone rower carrying his shell on his head, oars in his left hand:

Hi Denise, I'm in my room at the ninety minute break we get in between rowing sessions. Everyone else is at yoga, but I don't have the strength. We had a seven am row before breakfast—was so tired and cranky without food or caffeine that I nearly beaned one coach with my oar. Two more times to go today, and three tomorrow. What was I thinking? At least my legs are getting tanned, if only the tops of my calves.

XXX Emma

Email to Angela, from my Verizon Wireless BlackBerry:
Hey Angela—why didn't I just stick to kayaking? This is my third day of camp, and we have been on the water eight times. On the plus side I'm learning a phenomenal amount on technique, skills etc. These people are very serious. They eat, sleep, row for weeks at a time. I just can't get that intense about anything, especially not a sport. Yesterday they had us pile into the student center, and showed us several training films, plus the last few Olympics—eights and singles. Who wants to train for anything if it isn't fun? Who needs grueling? School is long over. Are equestrians this nuts? Riding is such a small part of what it takes to be a true horsewoman.

See you for lunch on Wednesday. I'll be the very brown, muscle bound female at the table by the window. Love, Emma

Journal entry for Sunday night:
Very grateful to be home! I blew off the final after breakfast row, packed my bags, and left, just as the others were walking (trudging) back to the boathouse. I had a leisurely lunch on the porch of the Norwich Inn in Vermont, and here I am.

Exhausted, sore, and missing Abby. Can't wait to pick her up tomorrow.

Why do people get so obsessed about sports? Football, hockey, skiing, sailing. It's all so nonsensical to me. One may get caught up in the energy of an exciting game, or race, but careers made or destroyed on one point? Or $1/100^{th}$ of a second? Who cares?

On the drive home today I was thinking about *Mutant Message Down Under*. The Real People in Australia didn't permit competition in their lives. They said that games were for fun, and how can someone have fun if they lose? I couldn't agree more. How silly it all seems, in light of what's happening on this planet. I don't want to roar across the lake in a racing shell. Nor do I want to careen around a jumper course on Joy. What's the rush? The pleasure is in the journey.

Look at what the drive to win does to people. Litigation lawyers are pompous windbags. They accomplish nothing beyond creating enormous fees for themselves. Politicians are even worse. I watched the coaches this weekend, and took note of their various styles. Bridget is a lovely, even tempered person, and my favorite part of the program was the backing and turning drills that we did with her. Philip, the grandpa, was gentle and positive—a real darling. A blatant contrast was Trevor's style: teach by shaming. After two days of his military command approach of barking orders at us, I'd had enough. When I finally lost it and blurted out "Do I work for you?" I knew I was in for abuse for the remainder of the week-end. Everything out of that guy's mouth is a back handed slap. Who needs to pay someone to put up with that kind of abuse? Enough.

Once I feel confident enough with rowing, I'm going to buy my own shell and haul it to various bodies of water on the top of my car. Eventually I want my own home on a lake. I'll go as fast as I like, in the direction that I choose. Down with lemmings.

CHAPTER 17

Fraud

"Is there any news on the *Garraty* case, Denise?"

"It's a possibility that the alterations originated in the hospital. How we prove that is another story. Vicky and George are working on this file exclusively."

"Any chance that the changes occurred in error?"

"None. Too much cut and paste on the originals."

Annie showed Marianne Sheehan into my office just before lunch the next day.

"The lawyer who's representing your brother and sister is playing games. I think he's banking on the fact that I don't normally handle probate matters. A mistake."

"What's he doing?"

"First, tell me about the piece of land that abuts your mother's house."

"It's a half acre. Utterly useless as a building lot."

"Why should your brother have an interest in it, then?"

"Oh the bloody boat. You remember the *Good Deal*. He took us for a ride around Candlewood Lake one summer."

"Does he keep the boat on this lot?"

"Yes, in a makeshift shed. The only way he gets to a have a slip in the marina is by owning property in the community."

"This lawyer, Gene Spencer, says that he'll encourage your sister to give you an advance on your grandmother's estate, if you agree to sign off on your mother's abutting parcel."

"That's extortion!"

"I made it quite clear that I would not allow you to be strong armed into losing part of your inheritance to get an early disbursement. I've already drafted a Motion to Compel."

"Thanks Emma. Why are they doing this to me? They both have plenty of money."

"Because they're controlling jerks? Some people really get a rush from hurting other people. I believe that mental health experts call them sociopaths. But there are ethical considerations as well. Your sister Shannon has a fiduciary duty as executrix of your grandmother's estate. I need to find out who the ring leader is."

"That's easy. My brother Brian. A nastier human being never lived."

Annie buzzed. "Em, your husband's on the line. Shall I take a message?"

"Please. Anyway Marianne, I think I can get a pretty speedy hearing date. What's your schedule like?"

"I'm completely open."

"Great. Let's do lunch. I could really use a chicken Caesar and a big ice tea."

Early the next morning I listened to a voicemail from Nick:

"Emma, you never got back to me yesterday. I need you to release the lis pendens on the house in Warwick so I can re finance to raise money to pay our lawyers. Kindly return this call."

I sent Donald Hall a quick email. It was less painful to pay Don, than to deal with Nick.

Annie appeared at my door and looked at me in sympathy. "Ready for more?"

"Now what?"

"Your friend Marianne again. She's in hysterics. Something about a toilet. Or maybe it was a bathtub."

"Oh Emma, I don't know what to do!"

"Your brother again?"

"NO! IT'S RALPH!"

"You need to stop howling at me Marianne. I'm getting a headache."

"Oh. Sorry."

"What happened?"

"I went to bed at around eleven. I got up at three to use the bathroom, and found him passed out, stark naked, on the commode."

"Did you wake him up?"

There was a pause. "Do you think I should have?"

Have mercy.

"Is that all that happened?"

"This morning I went back into the bathroom and found him in the tub."

"Still passed out?"

"No. This time he had a towel wadded up over his face. He said he wanted to drown himself."

"OK, Marianne. DID YOU REMOVE THE TOWEL?"

"YES! Then I called the police. They came with an ambulance and hauled him to the hospital."

"When did this happen?"

"A few hours ago. I need to get down there."

"Good idea. Keep me posted."

I was packing up to leave when Denise walked into my office, a deer in the headlights expression on her face.

She dropped into an arm chair. "I've had the day from hell, Em," Denise reported sadly. "It was George all along."

"George all along what?"

"And Vicky. And apparently, Vicky's husband."

Light dawned. "Oh God. You mean the *Garraty* mess? How did you find out?"

"Vicky's husband Justin is an anesthesiologist at the hospital. Somehow, he managed to get to Sonia Garraty's records and alter them. We've been investigating this matter for weeks. One of the people in his department tipped off the hospital administrator."

"But how did George get involved?"

"I guess he's over extended, like so many people these days, and he saw a chance to get a big settlement quickly. Vicky says it was his idea."

"What does George say?"

"He told me privately that he and Vicky were having an affair, that Vicky came up with the idea, and that she manipulated Justin into fiddling with the file. George is devastated, Em."

"He must be. Has the State's Attorney's office gotten hold of this yet?"

"Not as of five o'clock, but it's only a matter of time. I've been in a meeting with the partners in my old firm all day. We anticipate a state criminal investigation, at the very least."

"Insurance fraud."

"Oh yes. The entire firm will be under fire for this. Thank God I left when I did. What the *hell* was George thinking?"

"He probably wasn't thinking with his head, Denise. We deal with people like him all day long. What is George going to say to his wife and kids?"

"I don't know, but it's going to be agony, for all of them." Denise looked at me. "You knew all along, didn't you? About Vicky, I mean."

"I didn't *know*. She was caught cheating on our UCC exam in our second year. Everyone in the room that morning was sworn to secrecy. She managed to talk her way out of expulsion, and then she got her first job with a firm in New London, using a puffed up resumé. By the time her employers had caught on to her lack of credentials, or credibility, she and Justin had moved to D.C. I have also heard that there were several issues while she was still a nurse, one of which involved tampering with a patient's records. The patient had died. Of course, all this was years ago, but several of us in that UCC class have kept in touch."

Denise looked dumbfounded. "I should have listened to you from the start. You tried to tell me."

"It's all about character, Denise. You can wrap it up in charm and lies, but character always comes out in the end."

That night I dreamed that I am back in the master bedroom in Warwick with Nick. As usual, Nick is reading, while I am clinging to my side of the bed, so I don't accidentally touch him. Ginny is standing there, talking to me. She is wearing blue pajamas, and jewelry—a necklace, and fancy dangling earrings. Her dark hair is pulled back in a braid. She is chatting about her barn. "How is Joy doing?" She asks. She tries to explain her presence to Nick, but he is oblivious. "He can't hear you," I say. "This is telepathy, remember?"

CHAPTER 18

Suicide

The next morning I woke up, and decided to take my own shamanic journey to resolve the Ginny issue.

After the sun set, I lit a fire, and every candle in my library. With Sandra Ingerman's drumming CD playing in the background, I wrote down my intention, and then said it out loud. "What do I need to do to feel better about Ginny?" Then: "I wish to meet my power animals in the Lower World."

With these goals firmly fixed in my mind, I lay down on the floor, with a washcloth over my eyes.

When I am ready, I leave my body, and dive into Lake Washington. I fall through the water, watching fish swim by as I drop. I reach the bottom of the lake, and finally land in a dry cave. A red squirrel is sitting on a rock, twitching his tail. "Are you my power animal?" I ask. He shakes his head. A big black bear lumbers up to me. I ask her if she is my power animal. She points her enormous paw to the opening of the cave. I walk toward it. Outside is a beach, and the roaring sea. A huge seal is playing in the waves. I sit on the beach and watch. The seal dives, and comes up very near. He has an oyster, which he holds out to me.

Ginny sits on the sand next to me. She is dressed in black.

"Don't you love me any more?" She asks, with a pout on her face.

"I will always love you," I reply. "But now you have to help yourself. I can do no more for you. Everything you need to heal is on the website. It was mostly because of you that I created this group."

"I know," she says.

"Please do not bother me at night. It is my intention to block your energy from invading my luminous field ever again. You must take the steps to heal yourself."

Ginny isn't happy with this. She is still pouting. "OK," she says. She gets up and walks slowly down the beach. Her shoulders are hunched in her black jacket. I watch the seal play until it is time to return to my body.

Denise and I took a turn hosting a meeting of the Connecticut Affiliation of Professional Women at our office. Annie came in with us to take the minutes.

Denise asked Tracy O'Brien, CPA, to report on the recent talk some of our members had given at the Norwalk Library.

"We had about fifty attendees," Tracy said, "most of which were in the process of getting divorced, but there were a few retirees and one lesbian couple as well. Nan opened with a discussion on her role as a trusts and estates lawyer. She gave a basic explanation of the Probate Court system, and emphasized the importance of a well drafted estate plan, especially for gay couples. Rita took over, and described her function as a certified financial planner, and investment advisor. I covered tax and the different filing statuses. Jean talked about life and health insurance plans, and Carol enlightened the audience about credit reports and other necessaries required when one applies for a mortgage. We finished up with the divorce lawyer," Tracy chuckled, "as we assumed, rightly as it turned out, that most of the questions would be directed to her."

"Were they ever!" Stacy Harley, a new member from Darien, exclaimed. "I was hammered with free advice queries for nearly half an hour, until Tracy saved me. Most of them had to do with litigation problems, but a few wanted to know more about mediation. I referred those people to Denise and Emma. The women out there need a lot of help—I think the idea for this group is a godsend."

I privately agreed.

"At the end we handed out our individual materials, as well as the new group pamphlet," Tracy continued. "We encouraged the attendees to visit the CAPW site, and to read all of our articles."

"Our efforts were very well received," Carol added. "Not to mention profitable. I've had three calls already about refinances."

Jean nodded. "I've had several calls as well. It seems that women like to know that other women are on their side. It feels safe and comfortable, especially if one has had a bad experience with a man, in whatever capacity."

"Well done ladies!" Denise praised them. "This was only our second public speaking event, and the word seems to be out there."

I added: "Susan Cappelli, our PR person, does a terrific job getting CAPW press releases into the papers. We've just heard that the Darien paper is going to run a story about the group, showcasing Stacy as our newest member. Let's keep the momentum going."

"So what next?" Jean asked. "I was wondering about talking to high school students. You know, get them while they're young, hopefully before they've made big mistakes?"

"Excellent idea!" Randy replied. "I'd love to talk about the psychology of transitions from high school minor to college adult, and the pressures that come with that huge step."

"I could discuss career goals and putting together resumés for summer jobs," Liz said.

"Why don't we send out an email to the members who aren't here, or perhaps include an inquiry in this month's minutes?" I replied. "We have a number of high school age mothers in the group—parents who will have access to school boards and principals."

Lori came in and briefly whispered in Denise's ear.

"Sorry gang, I've got to take an urgent call from my old office," Denise announced. She and Lori hurried out of the room.

There was continued discussion regarding public relations for CAPW.

"Another piece of good news," I said, grinning. "Denise and I have been invited to be interviewed on two different radio programs, and one podcast. So for the next few weeks we'll be...."

Annie looked up. "Emma," she said quietly. Denise was walking toward us, her face a frozen mask. "I'm sorry everyone, but I have to leave immediately." She turned to me. "I'm afraid that George has committed suicide."

I have never worn black. This decision was a reaction to the fact that Audrey had hounded Kate and me from birth about little old Italian women and their inevitable mourning ensembles.

Dottie and I had attended George's funeral in support of Denise. Several hours later, we were foregathered at the home of our deceased host. Dottie was piling roast beef onto a poppy seed roll.

"These post obsequies get-togethers are depressing, aren't they?" She helped herself to a huge dollop of German potato salad.

"What are they called, anyway?" Denise wanted to know. "Receptions? Feeding frenzies?"

"I've never known," I replied, applying myself to curried chicken salad. "Have you seen the widow?"

"Just to issue the standard murmur of regret."

"She looks like she's on tranquilizers," Dottie observed.

"I would be too."

"That's the daughter over there." Denise said.

We regarded a rather beefy brunette with a huge nose and a crimson face, who was grasping a glass of white wine in her right hand and nodding emphatically at the small female in front of her.

"She's supposed to be a recovering alcoholic. Her brother went through drug rehab in high school."

"Quite the family, aren't they?"

"Wait till you meet the grandmother. On George's side."

Denise moved off to circulate with her former firm.

"Dorothy, has Denise spoken to you about coming to work for us full time?"

Dottie looked surprised. "No. Is she going to?"

I handed her a gin and tonic. "I'm doing it now, for both of us. Are you interested?"

"Of course!" She grinned. "I enjoy working at your office. A fresh start with like minded women is certainly appealing right now."

Five minutes later, Denise joined us for another drink and a quiet toast to our new team.

There was a commotion at the front door. Everyone stopped talking and stared as a small blond woman in spike heels pushed her way toward us.

"I can't believe it!" I exclaimed.

"Vicky Marshall," Denise breathed.

She was wearing a burgundy sleeveless dress with a plunging neckline and a very short hem. Her long hair was curled, her earrings sparkled, and her face was made up for a cocktail party. A Chanel bag swung from her left shoulder.

"There you are girls! I was hoping that you hadn't left yet." She surveyed the buffet. "Is there a shrimp platter anywhere?"

Denise opted for the high road. "There was. You missed it. How are you doing, Vicky?"

"Hanging in there. I've finally gotten rid of my husband, thank goodness."

I decided to take Denise's cue. "When is your trial, Vicky?"

"Don't know now. George's offing himself has messed up the timetable. Nothing I can control though. That's my lawyer's job. Assuming that he's doing it."

"Yes, well, it certainly was an inconvenient twist to things," Denise replied.

"George never was a strong guy. I had to do everything. He caved too easily." She gave us a lipless grin and popped an olive in her mouth.

"Oh dear," Denise whispered. "Here comes Grandma."

George's mother resembled a tugboat in black. "Mrs. Gardner," Denise began, "this is my law partner, Emma Carbury, and Dorothy Simko, our paralegal."

Mrs. Gardner's eyes barely glanced our way. "Thank you for coming." Her mouth quivered with repressed emotion. "Who is this with you?"

Vicky extended one of her small white hands, jangling bracelets on both wrists, nails an inevitable candy apple red.

"Victoria Marshall. Nice to meet you."

The tugboat appeared to swell. "How *dare* you! You're the reason that my son is dead!" I looked over to the other side of the room. George's wife, surrounded by cooing women, was sobbing on the blue damask sofa. The daughter was by the bar again. No sign of the son. "Do you *see* the state of his wife? *Leave this house at once.*"

Vicky replaced two olives on the tray with deliberation. "Listen, you ugly old toad. George came after *me*, OK? He said his wife was as cold as a witch's tit. At least he had some fun before he croaked." We all gaped at her. "And, by the way, he also said that his mother was a nasty old bulldog bitch." She adjusted her shoulder strap. "Ta ta, ladies." Her exit was punctuated by an impressive display of hip swaying.

Mrs. Gardner recovered her dignity and joined her granddaughter at the bar.

"Now, that was memorable," Dorothy said.

"Definitely stands out in my funereal archives," I agreed.

"Are we ready to head out?" Denise asked, looking a little shaky.

"Certainly. Do we say anything to the widow?" Over at the couch, the crowd had grown, and the sobbing had escalated.

"Better not."

"Well!" Dottie exclaimed. "Vicky may be going to jail, and disbarred, but she sure can shake up a room."

"Hmm." I said. "She'd better be careful. She's left a trail of destruction wherever she's been. At some point, her behavior will catch up with her."

Three days later, it did.

Denise came in to my office, a very odd expression on her visage.

"What's up?"

"You know how Vicky Marshall and her husband were scheduled to be pre-tried next week for insurance fraud, et cetera?"

"Yes?"

"Well, they're not going forward."

"Why not? Another stall tactic?"

"No. Lack of a defendant."

"What do you mean?"

"Vicky was found in her hot tub this morning, Emma. She's dead."

"So, are you going to the wake?" Annie asked me before court on Tuesday morning.

"I'll admit that I'm curious, but I'm sure it will be standing room only."

"Well, I'm going. Wouldn't miss it."

"Don't you think that's taking kind of a ghoulish approach to this tragedy?"

"What tragedy? I think of it more as divine intervention."

"Did Denise say if any decisions have been made on Vicky's trial?"

"Her husband will still have to face the music. By the way, guess who was prescribing her tranquilizers?"

"Her husband?"

"How did you know?"

"Seemed logical. Was the bottle dated? I'd be curious to learn if Vicky got the pills before or after her marriage split up."

"Denise said that the pharmacy filled the order last week." Annie looked at me. "You don't think that this was an accidental death, do you?"

"If I'm toying with the idea, I guarantee you that the police are already on to it. The trick would be to prove it."

Denise came in. "Full scale investigation," she announced. "I just heard. The husband has had to open up his records. They're searching for discrepancies."

I snorted. "What if the prescription was legit and he forced them down her throat?"

"Or up her butt, like they think happened to Marilyn Monroe?"

"Poor Vicky," Denise said, clearly shocked.

"Oh please!" Annie chortled. "The woman was a criminal and a home wrecker."

"So she deserved to drown in her own tub?"

"Well, they couldn't burn her at the stake, could they?"

I laughed.

"I wonder what they'll put her in?" Annie mused.

"What kind of box?"

"No. What kind of outfit. I bet it's that magenta leather number she always wore to Bar Association functions. With the diamond ankle bracelet and matching pedicure."

"Could be."

"Besides, if she parboiled in that water all night, they're going to have to get a little creative with the make-up."

"So true."

"Maybe all her hair fell out. Then, she'll be wearing a wig."

"Ugh!"

"I'll let you know." Annie grinned, slinging her bag over her shoulder.

CHAPTER 19

Justice

I met Angela on the second floor of the Dover courthouse. We had half an hour until her pretrial was due to start.

"What's this Judge Melnick like, Em? Is he going to be pro husband?"

"I honestly don't know. He was just appointed from the Hartford area, so I don't have a clue about his mindset."

Angela didn't look happy.

Dick Caxton, Angela's husband, stepped off the elevator, looked our way, and waved to Angela.

"Look at the smug faced jerk! What's he grinning about?"

"It's just a tactic, Angela. A pretty lame one, frankly. Still no sign of his learned counsel?"

"I saw him in the lobby. Maybe he's getting a cup of coffee."

"Or sacrificing a couple of virgins in the basement."

The clerk came out to find us just as Attorney Rocco Fugachi made his appearance. We secured our clients at a safe distance from each other in the courtroom, and followed the young woman through the courtroom and out the back door to the judge's chambers.

Judge Andrew Melnick was about my age. Tall athletic build, graying dark hair, nice features. He exuded reasonable professionalism. He extended his right hand to me first. "It's a pleasure, Ms. Carbury." No wedding ring on his other hand. Hmm.

Opposing counsel panted for attention. "Roc Fugachi, judge."

"Ah yes. I've heard all about this file from the Honorable Tuchman."

I relaxed. Judy Tuchman was dependably direct.

"Is your client employed, Attorney Fugachi?"

"Well, judge. We've run into some difficulties in that area."

"Such as?"

"Mr. Caxton has been unable to find a job that suits him."

"Attorney Carbury?"

"My understanding, your honor, is that the defendant has been made several lucrative offers from various universities. However, he has not been inclined to accept any of them. Apparently the locations were not ideal."

"Is that the case, Attorney Fugachi?"

"More or less, yeah, judge."

Judge Melnick turned to his clerk. "Get the reporter, will you Cheryl? I'm opening court." He pulled his robe off the coat stand in the corner. "Attorney Carbury, are you prepared to argue an oral motion for contempt?"

"Certainly your honor."

"Then I suggest that you both go out and prepare your clients. I'll give you ten minutes."

Fugachi pulled me aside as we walked back into the courtroom. "Shit! That bastard will send Caxton to jail."

"Did you advise him to take one of those offers?"

"Well...."

"You'll be lucky if the judge doesn't send *you* to jail," I replied breezily, and moved over to where Angela was sitting.

"What will happen?"

"I'll put you on the stand and ask you to testify as to what your husband told you about his lack of gainful employment. Fugachi will cross examine, not that he's got much of a chance of rehabilitating his client. Then, he'll put Dick on and try to make him smell like a rose. I get to cross after that, but my guess is that the judge will beat me to it. Your husband may be marched straight off to Bridgeport Correctional."

"That would be pretty awful, right?"

"The worst. I've heard some real horror stories. Let's hope that the judge has Plan B in mind."

The judge did.

"The court finds that the defendant, Richard Caxton, is in willful contempt of the order that was entered by Judge Tuchman. The defendant shall have one week—that's until next Tuesday at ten a.m., Mr. Fugachi—to provide proof of employment, or the defendant will be immediately incarcerated until such time as he has accepted a reasonable job offer. Do I make myself clear, Mr. Caxton?"

"Yes, your honor."

"I want to see both counsel in my chambers."

The judge went right for Rocco's throat. "Attorney Fugachi, your client has testified that he deliberately disregarded Judge Tuchman's order as a result of your advice. I am within seconds of filing a grievance against you myself. You'll be very fortunate if your client does not do so. This will not happen again. Understood?"

"Yes, your honor."

"I will see all four of you back here next week. Does that work for you Attorney Carbury?"

"It does, your honor."

The judge grinned at me. I felt a swoop in my solar plexus region.

"Good. Please tell my clerk to come in here on your way out."

I had lunch with Denise.

"It's too bad that Angela is going to have to wait even longer to unload this guy," she said, "but she must have had some satisfaction from Judge Melnick's tongue lashing."

I could feel my face turn red. "I know I did." I told her about my exchange with his honor.

"What is it with you and judges?" Denise exclaimed. "Do you have a thing about authority figures? Is it the black robe that turns you on? Or maybe the gavel?"

"I think it's the job that they do, frankly. They're not advocates. They're arbitrators. The best ones are wise and fair. And this guy is good, I can feel it."

"Uh huh." Denise smirked. "I'll bet he is. I know for a fact that the good judge was divorced about a year ago, so he's available. Do you think he'll call you?"

"I don't know. I sure hope so."

So much for Nick's lesbian theory.

Annie buzzed me later that afternoon. "Your friend Marianne called while you were on the phone."

I returned her call with misgivings.

"Oh Emma, thank goodness! The police were here again last night."

"Why?"

"Ralph's in violation of his restraining order. He was drunk and verbally abusive. Then he mouthed off at the cops, so they hauled him away."

"You can't keep using the police to get Ralph out of the house, Marianne. You need to get a divorce and move on."

"That's pretty much what they said last night. They asked for your number."

"Great."

"You know we don't have the money to live separately right now, Emma."

"Yes. But Ralph can't work from a jail cell."

"That *is* the difficulty."

"Well, I'll call the other lawyer in your probate case. Maybe I can light a fire under his butt to get your grandmother's estate closed faster, so we can get you some cash."

"That would really help."

"I thought Ralph made a good living as a landscape designer."

"He does. I just never see any of it."

"If you'd let me serve him with a divorce action, the court would order him to cover the household expenses."

"But then all the marital assets would be frozen. I couldn't sell my house without his permission."

"You could get a court order. Either way, losing your home in a foreclosure sale is hardly a solution."

The next day.

Annie buzzed. She sounded exasperated. "Marianne Sheehan, line one."

"Oh Emma, I've got a problem!"

"Did you have Ralph arrested again?"

"No. The judge said he had to move out. He didn't have any-where else to go, so he got a room at a hotel in town. The bad news is, Ralph used my ATM card to reserve the room, so now, after a week, my checking account is cleaned out and the hotel is threat-ening to sue us for the balance."

"Why would you give your bank card to your abusive husband?"

"Because the judge said...."

"I know what the judge said Marianne. Ralph still works, doesn't he?"

"Yes."

"So, why would you put yourself in such a position with a man who is utterly irresponsible, not to mention violent toward you?"

"I don't know!"

"There is also, unfortunately, the matter of your bill with this firm. The office manager tells me that you're two months behind."

"Things are very tight right now. Ralph is cashing his paycheck and squandering it instead of making payments."

"What about the twenty thousand dollar advance I got you from your grandmother's estate?"

"It's already gone."

"Did you pay your mortgage?"

"No, just the arrearage. The real estate agent said that I should put in new carpet and get new appliances if I want to get a good price for the house. I also got a new computer. The problem is, I can't afford the cable bill, so that got shut off. They're about to shut off the water."

"I see. You do seem to have issues with problem solving, Marianne. I really can't do any more work for you until our bill is paid."

"I'll be able to pay you when I sell the house," she cried.

"You have almost no equity, and there is the real estate commission. I'm sorry Marianne, but I'm charging you a lower rate than usual, as it is. I have a partner to answer to."

"I understand."

"Good. You might want to consider getting a job."

"Ralph's car is falling apart, and the bank is threatening to repossess mine. I have no way of getting around."

"Well, that's the best advice I can give you."

I walked over to Lori's office and handed her the file. "Would you please do a final invoice for this matter, and send it out?"

"Another legal leech?" Lori grinned. "Sure. Probably a waste of paper though."

"Yes," I agreed. "But the good news is, this is the last energy suck case that I'll ever take. Some people just don't want to help themselves."

CHAPTER 20

Nantucket

One of the many glories of Nantucket is that the island is pure beauty in every direction that one looks. Unlike the average vacation resort, where there is money, but often no charm, Nantucket has been preserved as a doorway to the past. Thirty miles off the coast of Massachusetts, the town contains the largest number of pre 1840 buildings in the United States, and the local authorities are fierce about maintaining its historical integrity.

Journal entry for Sunday night, September 6,
Nantucket Island:

I stood by the starboard railing yesterday afternoon as the Steamship Authority ferry rounded Brant Point and edged into Nantucket harbor. The long awaited feeling of serenity had already begun to instill itself. We docked, and I hurried down to the lower level to retrieve my luggage. In just a few minutes of walking through town, I was almost completely revived. The weather has been perfect—warm and breezy by day, and slightly chilly at night. Very glad that I remembered to bring my cashmere wrap.

There is such a soothing symmetry to the architecture here—gray shingles, white trim, roof walks—and the gardens! Huge purple hydrangeas, and roses everywhere, but the pervasive aroma is of honeysuckle. I can almost hear the carriage wheels on the cobblestones.

I'm spending the first night in town at the Scallop Inn on Orange Street. It was a captain's house, so wide plank floorboards, plaster walls, six over six windows, and historical trim colors. My room, the "Captain Starbuck," has a king four poster, a marble bathroom, gorgeous Oriental rugs, and a decent breakfast.

Tomorrow I move to Sconset, on the eastern side of the island—I've rented a cottage on the bluff over the beach until Sunday.

I wandered around town yesterday, and had dinner at an Italian restaurant on India Street—beet salad with goat cheese, and pasta with garlic and spinach in a cream sauce. I drank two glasses of sparkling wine, and enjoyed watching the passersby, and the light dancing in different colors on the cobblestones, as the sun went down.

The last two times I was here, it was with Nick. It's lovely to be back, on my own.

Vacations by oneself are heaven. Do what you want, when you want. Change your mind—your plans—as frequently as you please. Eat and shop whenever the mood strikes. Meet friendly people, chat for a bit, and then move on. I love the freedom. The key, I think, is to keep walking forward—don't just sit on your hill feeling terrified. Shake it up. Challenge yourself, every day. The satisfaction is enormous.

To celebrate my first night on the island, I took a guided ghost walk. When I arrived at six forty-five pm, there was already a crowd waiting on the sidewalk in front of the Atheneum, on the corner of India and Federal. Our guide announced that his name was Seth, and that he had lived on the island all of his life, which looked to be about sixty years. He cheerfully collected each person's fee and began herding us down the cobblestoned section of India Street.

We stopped in front of a white clapboard house on the right. It had the traditional stoop with steps on both sides. The mark of a well-to-do whaling captain, or so we were told.

"This building has seen some extraordinary activity," Seth began. "A young couple rented it three summers ago and left after only a couple of days. The story goes that they often heard loud conversations in the house, especially in the kitchen. Dishes and utensils would fly around, doors would open and close, drapes would be pulled across in front of them, there'd be heavy footsteps on the stairs. The last night, Mrs. Cole swore that a man sat on the bed with her and wouldn't allow her to get up. She said she felt as if she was suffocating."

There were several appreciative gasps at this point. Then, we turned right onto Centre Street and were halted before a large brick house with an impressive glass fanlight and two chimneys.

Seth had a definite flair for the dramatic. "See that corner window on the right?" He pointed. "That's where many sightings of the woman who originally lived here in the 1830s have occurred. Her husband lost everything in the Great Fire of 1846, and they were forced to sell their home." Seth paused for effect. "But she never really left."

We turned onto Hussey Street. The sun was gone completely, and the only light shone from old fashioned street lamps and the occasional front window. We clustered around Seth in front of a small, shingled building.

Out in the harbor, a ferry blew its long loud horn. It was a mournful sound, and it created excellent atmosphere.

"This was originally a Quaker meeting house, built in 1833. On very foggy nights," Seth grinned, "of which we have many on this island, one may still see the worshipers in their traditional attire assembling to enter this structure. I have observed them myself, on several occasions."

"It is said," he continued, in sepulchral tones, "that it is the cool, moist air on Nantucket that encourages the unusual amount of paranormal activity that we experience here."

"The same could be said of the British Isles, couldn't it?" a woman in particularly offensive apple green clam diggers asked.

"Yes, exactly. Perhaps the atmosphere is more conducive to manifestations."

We continued west on North Liberty Street toward Old North Cemetery.

Seth was winding up for his big finish. "Some of the oldest graves on Nantucket are here in this cemetery. Note those of the original families, Coffin, Macy, Starbuck, and Folger. Many islanders and tourists have been witnesses to ghostly appearances here."

He walked over to a particularly ancient looking stone, and aimed his flashlight at the carving. "Here, for example, lies

Abraham Johnson. Born 1716, died 1769. At that time, the island was still called Sherburne. Johnson and his family spent several hard years trying to farm the sandy soil near Siasconset, and finally relocated to what is now the town, where he took up carpentry."

"Has he been seen lately?" A high school boy in a letterman's jacket asked.

"He's one of our regulars," Seth replied. "And over this way is Maria Worth, one of the so-called independent women that Nantucket was famous for during the height of its whaling era. She was influential in promoting the Quaker faith on the island. It is said that she still presides over meetings right here at her grave."

"This stone, to my mind, is one of the saddest. Little Obed Mayhew, just seven when his father went off to sea in 1796, died six months later. Obed may still be seen, standing on this hill, looking out toward the harbor, waiting for his father to return from the Pacific. He never did."

As much as I loved Nantucket, the thought of spending a winter on the Atlantic Ocean, with no electricity or insulation, and few trees to block the wind—I felt even more grateful for my cashmere wrap, and twenty-first century comforts.

> *Journal entry for Tuesday, September 8, Siasconset:*
> Good surf! I'm sitting on the Sconset beach after lunch. Not a soul around except one lone seagull. It's windy, and overcast, and wonderful. I'm on a little dune, surrounded by rosa rugosa, Queen Anne's lace, golden rod, and some scraggy look-ing pines. There's a plant here that looks like yel-low loosestrife, but according to the book that I bought on Nantucket wildflowers, it may be Swamp Candles, which is in the primrose family. There are also a few bayberry bushes. I remember

those family summers on Cape Cod, collecting bayberries to make candles. I loved the waxy blue-gray color, and the aroma.

My cottage is perfect. The interior is a little shabby, especially in the kitchen, but the living room, bedroom and deck all face the sea, and I can hear the roar of the waves at night, even with the windows closed. I try to keep them open, though, if only just an inch. I enjoy watching the white curtains billowing with sea breeze. There are stairs down from the lawn to a path to the beach. I prefer staying on the Atlantic, on the eastern most part of Nantucket. You want the beginning of the day here to start as early as possible. I'm finding that I leap out of bed at 6:30 every morning, something I never do at home. I don't want to miss a minute on this island.

Last night I had a lovely dinner at the Sconset Inn Grill. I had them bring me three appetizers all at once: arugula salad with shaved parm, cherry tomatoes, and candied walnuts; three crab cakes, and a cheese platter with cranberry chutney. I drank two glasses of New Zealand chardonnay, and watched the light slowly disappear over the water. I assume that they watch the sun set out in Madaket. The walk back in the dark was magic.

Safe. I feel safe here. I'm very grateful to the five ladies who asked me to join their table at the restaurant, and the gentleman on Orange Street who was worried that I needed help with my suitcase. People are kind and happy here, and so are their dogs.

Postcard to my sister Kate, picture of a row of rose covered cottages in Sconset on the front:
Hi! I've done a little bit of shopping, since the end of season sales are so good. Got a sea foam green nightie with white lace trim to celebrate my new independence. Also a straw hat with a pink and white ribbon, and a tiny oil painting of Steps Beach. The seafood here is phenomenal, and the air is invigorating. There are always people who want to chat, so I am never lonely. In fact, I'm reveling in being on vacation by myself, for the first time in my life. Send me a text if you want beach plum jam. Love, Emma.

Email to Angela, via my BlackBerry:
It just doesn't get better than this Ange! I'm on a chaise, at the very edge of the lawn. It drops away, a good 20 or 30 feet, so I'm looking down on the tops of bushes and weather beaten evergreens, to sand paths that curve through the waving grasses, to the huge expanse of sea. I can hear the surf, but I can't see it breaking. The rose hips are very red at my feet. Two cottages with roof walks are to my right. One has heavy wooden shudders closed over the windows. I can see why—next stop is Portugal!

Journal entry for Wednesday, September 9,
Siasconset:

Spending the afternoon on the beach, with my
new English mystery, and my watercolors. The
sun is strong, and there's a refreshing breeze, but
the water is much too chilly to swim. The clouds
look like white cotton that has been stretched too
thin.

A huge seal played by himself in the surf for a
while. At one point he caught some sort of crea-
ture to eat, but I was too distressed to get a closer
look.

I've been thinking about the conversation that I
had with my cab driver out here from town. He
said that there has never been a problem with
potable water on Nantucket, in the twenty years
that he's lived on the island. He told me that the
people at the recycle center are very committed
to their jobs, and that they also generate compost
from paper and wood chips. He commented that
there is never litter on Nantucket, because people
pick up after themselves.

I now realize that people who attract abundance,
and want to enjoy a place like Nantucket, keep
everything beautiful because they understand
respect for the land, and the sea. Is it monetary
value that matters to them, or the spirit of the

place—or both? All of the beaches are open to the public here, unlike Martha's Vineyard, or most of the Connecticut coastline. And yet, Nantucket's beaches are gorgeous, wild, and everyone wants them to remain so.

There was an article in the island real estate magazine about Nantucket's surrounding seas—they're in astoundingly good shape, apparently, and the locals work very hard to maintain the health of the wildlife, and the cleanliness of the water. They are very aware of the rising sea level, and what it could do to the island.

I feel that a place that is as loved and protected by so many people as Nantucket can survive anything.

Journal entry for Thursday, September 10, Nantucket town
I was having breakfast at the café in Sconset, when the shuttle pulled up on the other side of the square. I decided on an impromptu trip to town.

The shuttle ride takes twice as long as the trip by taxi, but is a fraction of the cost. I was interested in seeing more of the interior of the island, where the locals live, and work, and shop. Interesting— the homes and businesses, although certainly less posh than those on the water, were just as well kept, and their owners clearly just as respectful of the natural beauty of Nantucket.

My first stop was to Claire Murray, on Federal Street, to take advantage of the sale on bath products. I bought bath salts in sea lavender, and had an interesting talk with the elderly woman who was behind the counter. She noticed the English mystery tucked under my arm, and what ensued was a lively discussion which ranged from modern novels, to Christian Scientists and their aversion to the medical profession. I recommended *Mutant Message Down Under*—explaining how miraculous the tribal members' homeopathic methods were. In turn, she suggested that I pick up a copy of William Shawcross's official biography, *The Queen Mother*. Apparently Queen Elizabeth was a believer in alternative health practices, and as she lived an impressively active one hundred and one years, I was inclined to take this woman's advice.

In fact, I found a paperback copy at the Nantucket Bookworks, and I am sitting in the garden at the Atheneum, flipping through the photographs. What a life! Born in 1900, Her Majesty experienced every moment of the twentieth century, and like Eleanor Roosevelt, was an icon of feminine power and stability. I stopped at the picture of the two women together in D.C. in 1939. I am determined to finish my novel tonight, so that I can start on the Queen Mother tomorrow.

I looked into the Nantucket Art Association on Orange Street on the way back to the shuttle stop.

I bought a (rather large) wood sculpture of a blue whale for my foyer in Southport, and had the gallery ship it. I have only been once to the Whaling Museum on Broad Street—it's wonderfully informative, but I can't bear the horrible harpoons and paintings of whale hunts. Those lovely, docile creatures! My sympathies are entirely with Moby Dick.

The new blue whale (name of Fred) is a testament to their honor.

Postcard to law partner Denise, picture of the "Rainbow Fleet" of sail boats, flying past Brant Point lighthouse in front:
Today I was sitting on the edge of the water to cool off—and I do mean cool—and picking up some interesting stones, when my buddy the big seal popped up just a few feet in front of me. My god he's huge!! We were both equally shocked. I squealed and jumped up; he started and dived under the waves again. He surfaced farther along the shore, and immediately checked to see that I was now a safe distance away. How I love this island! You may have to drag me back to the office on Monday, sand between my toes. XXX Emma

Journal entry for Friday, September 11, Siasconset:
I've felt for weeks that this was going to be an important trip for me, and now I know why. I have been coming to Nantucket on and off for nearly twenty years, but this is my first visit alone,

as an independent, free woman. I want a second home here.

It takes a few days to unwind when you start a vacation. I knew that on our trips to the lake house in New Hampshire, and was always grateful that my belongings were already up there: in my drawers, my closets, and my bookshelves, so I packed very little, very quickly. Most of the shopping was done in CT, and hauled north in coolers and L.L. Bean bags.

It would be tougher to do that here. I spent the morning musing on the logistics of cars and ferries, and then transportation on the island. It is definitely complicated, but doable. The most important thing is to think positively, and to eradicate all feelings of doubt and fear. This is so much easier to accomplish when you know exactly what you want.

I had a dream last night. A big playful blue and white kitten—and I am not much of a fan of felines, crawled into one of my shirts and pranced around in it. It was a funny dream, and I woke up laughing. I've gotten snippets of the good feelings that I used to have on the family vacations to Cape Cod. These trips ended around the time I was twelve, and although I don't white wash the bad stuff, I can still smell the roses that always grew over the split rail fences, and the deep green of the perfectly kept lawns—see the short sandy walk down to the beach. There were always pine needles mixed in the sand. I don't remember hydrangeas so much. Just the roses. And the old cottages: the white or green, or sometimes blue trim on weathered shingles, with names like "Shore Leave," "Sea Spray," and "Dune Cottage" carved on boards like they used to be on boats. The clang of the rope on the flagpole, and always the rumble of the surf in the background.

I'm sitting on my porch, which is framed by wisteria vines (must be gorgeous with fat purple flowers in the spring). I'm watching as huge black masses are moving south under the surface of the water—moving very fast. Schools of fish? Seaweed? There's a breeze, and little whitecaps dot the green water. I like to imagine that the whitecaps are dolphins, leaping about, following the fish. Do dolphins come this far north? I have no idea.

On Saturday morning, my last full day on Nantucket, I went to the café as usual for my breakfast, and ice coffee. The same sparkly fresh faced brunette was there, taking orders. I asked her if she was looking forward to leaving after the store closed for the season in a few weeks.

Her face clouded a little. "No," she replied. "I'm from here."

There was no one else in the café, and she just started talking. She went to boarding school in Massachusetts, and then to college on the West Coast, where she'd met her boyfriend. They've been together for five years. She explained that he had a graduate degree in engineering, and that he wanted to move to New York City to look for work.

I couldn't help myself. "You want to leave this beautiful place to live in Brooklyn?" I asked, incredulous. "That's where I'm from originally."

It became clear that she didn't want any part of this plan, but there was nothing for her on the island in the winter. Then she paused. "But it's so peaceful here, once the tourists leave." She went to school for psychology, and she was contemplating graduate school. She'd like to work with children, she said.

So of course I gave her unsolicited advice. "You have to take care of you first. Go with your gut, and never, ever live in sacrifice," I grinned, "even if the sex is really good. This I learned the hard way, now on my second divorce. It seems to me, if you're this conflicted, that something is very wrong."

She seemed grateful. Maybe this young woman had been waiting for some kind of clarification, because her ambivalence was obvious. I know what Afton would say: that this decision was a big cross road in her life, and I was there at the right time to help.

I never did learn the girl's name, and I avoided going back there for lunch, just in case she resented my interference, and decided to hit me with something.

> *Journal entry, Saturday night, 7pm:*
> The sun is going down, and the sky is layers of
> blue and pink.
>
> I'm glad to be going home. I miss my animals,
> and having the use of my own comfortable things.
>
> I will miss the sound of the sea. Unlike my surf
> CD, the crashing waves do not click off after fifty

minutes here, although there are occasional silent lulls, as though someone has hit the pause button.

Tonight it's very chilly, the windows are closed, and I am curled up with my new biography; very refreshing after the deadly perils in Devonshire that I've been reading. What a plot!!!

- Incest between two brother and sister pairs, in two different families
- Euthanasia: wife/husband
- Son burns parents in their home, then later sister burns same brother
- Baby swapping
- Body swapping
- Vicar pays parishioner for sex
- Same parishioner is sexually abused by her own husband
- Teenage pregnancy—fear of more incest, but thankfully not so
- Witchcraft
- Gay curate in love with brother of incestuous relationship/parent burning
- At least five murders, including the aforementioned curate
- Abuse of several animals, including a horse, a dog, and lots of birds
- Suicide

What busy people the Brits are! Reading this novel was like watching three seasons of Inspector Barnaby in one sitting.

Journal entry for Sunday night, September 13,
back home in Southport, CT:

I have had a lavender sea salt bath, Gregorian chants are playing on the CD player, and I have built my first fire of the season. It has been popping and hissing for several hours now, filling the room with wonderful aromas, and I am already a third of the way through the life of the Queen Mother. Her Majesty is my new role model. She lived a long, happy, productive century, full of family support, adventure, challenge, and above all, a full enjoyment of life. She loved the outdoors and her animals, she stood by her friends, and she carried out her state and charitable duties with a constant cheerfulness which never failed to charm.

We need more people of her caliber on this planet. Frankly, I would like more of them in my life. There have been too many upsets lately; I feel that I have to exercise ceaseless vigilance—people are almost never as they seem.

My vacation is over, and I look forward to returning to Nantucket soon. But now I have to really concentrate on the next few months: the depositions, the trial, and the aftermath of the divorce. Perhaps I can draw on the kind of spirit that Queen Elizabeth always showed to the world, even when prospects were darkest.

I just have to keep smelling those roses.

Mencken

The Book Club met at Dottie's for the September meeting. She had set out an assortment of appetizers: shrimp, spinach in phyllo dough, and little goat cheese pizzas.

Eliot sashayed in the door, bearing four bottles of chilled sparkling wine. "Jeff got a case for my birthday party," she explained. She began to pop corks.

"All right. Mencken. Who was he?" Angela asked.

"Henry Louis Mencken," Denise read from her notes. "Born in Baltimore in 1880. Departed this life in 1956, also from Baltimore. He was a journalist, a satirist, and a critic. He wrote for the *Baltimore Sun* for over forty years. He was opposed to the New Deal, and the United States' involvement in World War II, and he despised Franklin Roosevelt."

"His father was German," Eliot added.

"Suppose each of us chooses an essay from his *Chrestomathy* and discusses it?" Dottie said.

"I want to talk about his chapter on Women," replied Eliot, who was pouring.

We each took a glass.

"He likes women better than men," pronounced Eliot, with a slight burp. She was obviously ahead of the group by at least half a bottle.

"Can you expand on that comment?" Angela asked.

"Mencken says that men are such egotists that they confuse memorizing petty details with intelligence. He concludes that women are the real brainiacs—men merely regurgitate boiler plate facts and expect applause. There you are!" Eliot exclaimed, triumphant. "I love this man!"

"How long have you been married, Eliot?" Denise asked.

"This time? Two years. Why?"

"Listen to this!" I chortled. "He points out that every serious female novelist since Jane Austen has not so subtly created male heroes who are boobies."

"He moves on to American women in particular," Dottie said. "The reason we are such terrible cooks in this country, Mencken writes, is because women are bored by the mundane nothingness of housework. He says that our rebellion is a testimonial to our intelligence."

"I'm good with that," Eliot replied. "No argument here."

"Mencken explains that it's no coincidence that we evolved American women live in the land of canned soup and ready made food," Angela read.

"I feel completely validated for the take out dinners I buy," Denise said.

"I agree with him on the general subject of the drudgery involved with homemaking," I replied. "But the ability to produce culinary masterpieces is a real art."

Eliot rolled her eyes. "Most professional chefs are men, Emma. I like what Mencken writes about so-called women's intuition," she announced. "His theory is that men can't admit that we are smarter that they are, so they have invented an other-worldly talent and have named it intuition. He says that it is women who are the 'supreme realists' of our race. "

"Who's next?" Angela asked.

"I'll take Government," Dottie said. "I like the tie-in between this book, and what we covered in our discussion of *Franklin and Winston* last winter, especially in light of Mencken's much publicized opposition to the war."

"I'm surprised that he wasn't vilified for sedition," Denise remarked.

"He wasn't inciting riots, or passing secrets to the enemy," Angela the journalist replied. "The U.S. Constitution guarantees Americans the right to speak their minds. It's a free country."

"Not according to Mencken," Dottie said, drily. "He says that any government is going to be terrified of a citizen who ignores the bilge that is propaganda, and thinks for himself. Why? Because a smart public will come to the obvious conclusion that its government is dishonest and insane. Mencken points out that political revolutions never bring in change for the better, it's just more of same, under a new label."

"It's all about crushing the people who actually analyze what is going on," Eliot said, surprisingly. "Obviously, the folks who are running things don't want everyone else figuring out what they are really doing. So, the government tries to distract us."

"Distract us from what?" Denise asked.

"Mencken says that the government's motive is pure exploitation," Dottie explained. "He writes that no one actually believes that our taxes are used for anything of benefit to Americans."

"I love this line," I added. "He describes government as a kind of Big Brother to the American. It hovers over us with ceaseless vigilance, ever on the alert to squeeze us for more money. He defines politicians as predatory and useless."

Psychic vampires on the national scale.

"It's astonishing that these essays were written in the early part of the last century," Angela observed, "and yet they still have so much meaning today. Mencken concludes that government has become too strong to be safe. He likens citizens to subjects, saying that we work harder and harder, and more and more are dying for some cause or other, while all the while, we are benefitting less and less."

"But what's the alternative?" Eliot asked.

Dottie flipped through the essay. "Mencken writes that the solution, the ideal government, leaves the public alone, and is barely a government at all. That sounds wonderful," she commented. "But someone has to keep up the roads, pay the post man, and protect our borders. Does he suggest that we privatize all of these services?"

"That's a good question," Angela answered. "Maybe the problem isn't so much the concept of government, but the people to whom we give our power."

We sat in silence for a few moments.

Then Denise said: "I'd like to discuss Mencken's theories on 'Quackery.' Basically, he supports every American's right to consult any healer that he or she chooses. Mencken uses Christian Science practitioners as an example, but any off the beaten path theory is applicable here."

"Again, he is worried about the suppression of free thinking," I noted. "This stuff is a little out of date, since I doubt that many states forbid alternative health practices, if at all."

"Maybe not," Angela replied, "but does your insurance policy cover Reiki, or Aromatherapy, or your sessions with the Shaman? It's all about lobbying, and drug companies have huge power in Congress."

"A shaman would say that by constantly terrifying the public with diseases, or dis-eases, as they call them, the medical profession is actually giving energy to illness. Consider the ubiquitous pink ribbons—people mean well there, I suppose, but in reality it's more fuel for the medical community. This in turn suits the drug companies perfectly. Not to mention the hospitals, the companies who make medical equipment, et cetera."

"Again, what's the alternative?" Eliot demanded.

"My energy research claims that the focus should be on health, and maintenance of healthy lifestyles in all areas—physical, mental, and spiritual."

"Huh," Eliot replied. "So if we all do this weird stuff that you do, we'd all stay healthy, and we wouldn't need the medical profession?"

"How else do you explain that I've gotten through leaving my awful marriage, and this volatile divorce, as well as starting my own practice, without so much as one tranquilizer, or even a case of the sniffles?"

"Point taken," Angela said.

"On that note, I'd like to talk about the South," I volunteered. "Recall that I attended Vanderbilt University, which is in Nashville, Tennessee. At a time when young men still bought corsages for their dates to football games."

"Honestly?" Eliot asked.

"And if you weren't dating the right boy from the proper fraternity, you weren't going to get pinned and have a candlelight ceremony at your Monday night sorority meeting. Such was a defining moment in one's college career."

"So much for feminism in the eighties!" Denise exclaimed.

"Presumably things have changed in over twenty years. However, I would like it to go on record that I dated mostly non Greek guys—that is to say, not affiliated with a fraternity—and the first and only time I was pinned was after Nick and I were married." I paused. "I have since returned it to him.

"Mencken characterizes the South as a culturally and intellectually sterile desert—a dried up civilization. Once again, Mencken is concerned that Americans have lost the ability to think for themselves."

Angela continued: "He claims that the South died in the Civil War. I wonder what happened?"

"The Southerners had to free their slaves, that's what," Eliot remarked, pouring herself another glass. "No more time to sit around on the veranda and ponder the Universe."

"Mencken lauds those cities in the North that experiment with ideas," Angela continued. "He concludes that there is no such impulse in the South."

"He writes that all that remains of the ancient Southern tradition is a superficial, charming civility," Dottie noted.

"I used to ride with a Southern gal," I mused. "Mother of two small boys. Watching her at work, it was like being transported back to my junior year."

"What do you mean?" Eliot asked.

"She needed to be the center of attention in every conversation; to captivate every male within eye-batting range. She had every inch of her body artificially, and expensively, processed. But, make no mistake. These women are not stupid; far from it. They have been fooling men for decades."

"Yes, by playing the frailty card," Angela said, thoughtfully. "I see that as a disempowerment, of sorts. Regardless of their role as Steel Magnolias, I feel that women who behave this way are objectifying themselves, and doing a disservice to all women."

"What about the entertainment industry?" Dottie pointed out. "Movies, books. The last three novels I read all had to do with abuse of women and children. Two of them involved abuse of animals, as well. Do the people who put this junk out there think that they are helping? Do they imagine that they are enlightening the public, somehow?"

Eliot snorted. "Of course not! They're analyzing the market to see what sells, and they are selling it."

"And thereby giving the problem renewed energy," Dottie concluded.

Psychic vampirism on a global scale.

"Remember when the Princess of Wales was killed?" Angela asked. "The paparazzi all agreed to withhold any pictures of her in the crash. It was a step in the right direction."

"It was," I agreed. "But I would have been more impressed if those photographers hadn't been so concerned with future sales."

"I'd like to see the public put a general ban on any media that profits from victimization," Dottie remarked. "A *public* ban, mind you. Nothing whatever to do with the government. The public should exercise free will as to its chosen morality."

"I want to discuss Mencken's essays on Religion," announced Angela. "He agrees with the ancient Greeks that the Universe is run by a board of gods, all of whom have equal influence and authority."

"Sounds more like our own beloved government," Denise remarked. "The balance of power theory."

"I've got some sparkling left!" Eliot gurgled. Dottie held out her glass.

"He likens religion to poetry," I noted. "He says that science takes a bite out of religion on a daily basis, but the superficial coating of logic in religion merely makes it more palatable, even to intellectuals. Like poetry. And poets are morons, according to Mencken. I must admit, I have never taken to reading poems."

"Apparently Christians are the biggest morons of them all!" Angela said. "He argues that of all the other religions, Christianity will survive because it is moony and sentimental, and therefore appealing. Rather a circular argument, wouldn't you say?"

No one responded. I have always found that adults who still buy into the religious dogma which was hammered into them as children are afraid to question it, even after half a century or more. They have been brainwashed by fear.

"Here's one for you, Emma!" Eliot was clearly destined for a night on her bathroom floor. "Did you read the chapter on 'Lady of Joy'? That's what he calls prostitutes!"

"The bit that talks about hookers liking their jobs, and how most of them ended up married to men who are much higher in station?"

"Well yeah, but get this: Mencken says that hookers are better off than most women—their work is easier and less monotonous, and they meet a greater variety, and a better class of men."

"Amen to that!" Denise exclaimed.

"Who wants to go next?" Angela asked.

"I think we need to start organizing rides home," I said. Eliot was slumped over the arm of the sofa, and Denise was working on her third attempt to get out of her armchair.

"Super logical," Eliot muttered in her sleep.

CHAPTER 22

Deposition

Don Hall met me in the parking lot at Dunkin Donuts, just off the interstate in Darien. He handed me a large ice decaf with whole milk, and no sugar. "Now remember the signals, Em. If I throw down my glasses, I want you to shut up. If I start rustling papers, I'm trying to distract McAfee."

What was this? Kindergarten?

"First of all, you will never need to shut me up, Donald." He grinned. "Second, I can distract McAfee all by myself, thanks. He's got the brain power of a two watt bulb."

"True, but don't let him get to you. He'll be watching your body language. But then, I'm sure that most men are."

Somebody please tell me why I had to be here on the planet for this.

"Not to worry," I said, shortly. "After nearly twenty years in the practice of law, I think I can handle it."

We assembled in Michael McAfee's conference room.

"Let's deal with the Stipulations," the Court Reporter said. "It is hereby stipulated and agreed by and between counsel representing the respective parties that each party reserves the right to make specific objections at the trial to each and every question asked and of the answers given thereto by the deponent, reserving their right to move to strike out where applicable, except as to such objections as are directed to the form of the question.

"It is further stipulated and agreed by and between counsel representing the respective parties that proof of the official authority of the Notary Public before whom this deposition is taken is waived.

"Filing of the Notice of Deposition with the original transcript is waived.

"Reading and signing of the deposition transcript was requested."

I was sworn in. I sat back, crossed my legs, and smiled graciously at the idiot who was representing my husband.

Michael McAfee asked questions regarding my age, my educational background, my previous short marriage, my employment history since law school, my health, and my mental health. He asked about my expenditures for Reiki, aromatherapy, and Shamanic healing. He tried to get me to call my sessions with Marilyn and Afton psychotherapy, but I sidestepped him neatly.

"Are you currently employed?"

"I'm self employed."

"When did you set up your practice?"

I decided to have a little fun. "My practice?"

"Don't you have a law practice with Denise Frederickson?"

"Is that the question?"

"Yes."

"Yes."

McAfee began to look flustered. "Then when did you open your practice?"

"November first of last year."

"So almost a year?"

"Just about."

"And at that time, did Mr. Bennington give you forty thousand dollars?"

"I have a problem with the word 'give'."

"Did you receive forty thousand dollars?"

"Mr. Bennington disbursed marital assets of forty thousand dollars to me to open my practice."

"What did you do with these funds?"

"I bought furniture, I bought equipment, I bought stationery, and I paid rent."

"What is the nature of your practice today?"

"I do family mediation and collaborative divorce, and I still have a few family litigation files. I am review counsel for other mediators, I do second opinions on separation agreements. I take civil litigation and civil mediation files."

"I read an article that you have written about this networking group that you have with various people who work together?"

"Is that a question?"

"It's yourself and who?"

"Is what myself and who?"

"Do you have a name for your group?"

"Do I have a group?"

"Do you have a name for your group?"

"Yes."

McAfee let out a long breath. "And what's the name of that group?"

"Connecticut Affiliation of Professional Women."

"Does one have to pay a membership fee to become part of this group?"

"One pays one hundred and fifty dollars a year."

"And, I take it, the group refers clients back and forth?"

"Correct."

"What is your business income at this time?"

Donald woke up. "Objection. Is the question regarding gross receipts, taxable income, or income after taxes?"

"Gross receipts."

"I have no idea."

"What about taxable income?"

Don again. "You have her affidavit in front of you Mike."

"Is this calculated weekly, or monthly?"

"It's monthly," Don replied, a note of impatience in his voice.

"Have you considered seeking other employment through a law firm other than just your partnership?"

"No."

"And why not?"

"Because I'm done working for other people."

"Do you expect that your business income will increase?"

"Absolutely."

"Other than your law practice, are you doing anything else to generate income?"

"No."

"You were married to Nick Bennington on June third, twelve years ago, is that correct?"

"Correct."

"At that time, what assets did you have?"

"I had some furniture, some jewelry, and a Ford Mustang."

"Can we agree that at the time you were married that Nick Bennington owned the property in Warwick, Connecticut?"

"Certainly."

"And can we agree that he owned that property from 1980 onward?"

"I don't know that."

"Can we agree that he also owned a home in New Hampshire at that time?"

"What time?"

"At the time of your marriage?"

"Yes."

"And he purchased that property sometime in 1985?"

"I don't know that."

"What financial contribution did you make to pay mortgages, heating expenses, house expenses, for either of those properties over the course of your marriage?"

"I don't know how to answer that."

"Did you contribute any money from the time you were married through the time you were separated last year for the mortgage on the house in Warwick, Connecticut?"

"I don't know how to answer that."

"Did you give him any cash to pay the mortgage?"

"No."

"Did you give him any cash to pay household expenses?"

"No."

"Did you contribute anything at all to this marriage?"

"Objection," Don said, throwing down his glasses. Was that a signal? "The statute gives broad leeway to the term 'contribution,' as hopefully you know. Rephrase the question."

"All right!" McAfee barked. Sweat was breaking out on his forehead. "Question withdrawn. Were you employed at the time of your marriage to Nick Bennington?"

"Yes."

"And did you and Mr. Bennington come to an agreement as to the financial arrangement at that time?"

Finally. "Yes."

"What was that arrangement?"

"I would pay my own expenses from my salary. Nick would continue to cover the two houses, as his salary was at least three times what mine was at that time. My job was to manage the two homes, indoor and outdoor, holiday celebrations, our social calendar, any business socializing, our travel, our dogs, and any gift giving that was required."

"How was the horse purchased?"

"Objection to the form of the question," Don replied.

McAfee sighed. "Do you own a horse?"

"Yes."

"How much did the horse cost?"

"Twenty thousand dollars."

"Who paid the twenty thousand dollars?"

"I did."

"With your husband's consent?"

"Objection."

"Did your husband know that you were going to spend this sum on the purchase of an equine?"

"Yes."

"Where was the horse stabled at the time of the purchase?"

"Green Gates Farm in Redding, Connecticut."

"How much was the annual cost of stabling the horse at that location?"

"I believe it was twenty-five hundred dollars a month for board and training."

"Why was the horse moved from that location?"

"I had a falling out with her trainer."

"What was the nature of the falling out?"

I laughed. "His wife was jealous of the fact that he had a crush on me."

"Did you ever have an affair with him?"

"No."

"Was there any legal intervention in Redding to have you removed from the stable?"

"No."

"Did you ever get into a confrontation at the stable that led to any type of police involvement?"

"No."

"Where is the horse stabled now?"

"She's at Running Fox Farm in Fairfield."

"Do you intend to keep this horse?"

"Yes."

McAfee leaned forward. "And why is that?"

"I love her."

"Let me ask you this. Do you think that it's Mr. Bennington's responsibility to pay for your horse?"

Don was obviously prepared for this question. He huffed and puffed. He threw some paper around. Do clients actually buy into this act? "Objection to the form. Are you asking in the future?"

"In the future."

"Are you asking her to negotiate with you?"

"No, I'm asking...."

"I think, Mike, that in essence that's exactly what you're doing. You're trying to find out what my client's claims for relief are."

"It's a perfectly fair question."

Don puffed some more. "No. Her lawyer is the one who figures out what her claims for relief are in conjunction with this dissolution action. I will not have you negotiate with her."

Mike looked sulky. "She's a lawyer."

Don in turn looked offended. "Not today, she isn't. She's my client."

McAfee flipped through some exhibits, clearly aggrieved. Then he tried a new tack:

"Ms. Carbury, to what do you attribute the breakdown of your marriage?"

"Two things."

"Go ahead."

"First, Nick was extremely controlling with money. Second, I felt that our sex life was completely unsatisfying."

"At what point in the marriage did you feel that your sex life was completely unsatisfying?"

"Practically from the beginning. But I kept trying."

Donald smirked.

"Did there come a time in your marriage that you told your husband that you were not going to have any sexual relations with him?"

"No."

"When did you stop having sexual relations with him?"

It was more like a rape, but I merely replied, "a few months before I moved out. A little over a year ago."

Don grinned. "I guess she *did* keep trying, Mike."

McAfee used both hands to push his thinning gray hair back. "And during the course of your marriage, did you have any sexual relations with any other man?"

"No."

"How about with a woman?"

"No."

"Do you know a Virginia Sherman?"

"I did at one time, yes."

"When was this?"

"From November of last year until the end of February of this year."

"How did you meet Ms. Sherman?"

"She was training my horse for the winter."

"Were you attracted to her?"

"No."

"Virginia Sherman is the daughter of whom?"

"I have no idea."

"Isn't her father Douglas Sherman, CEO of Sherman Pharmaceuticals?"

"I don't know that."

"Did her family ever tell you to stay away from Virginia?"

"No."

I was aware of the extreme irony of the situation. Here I was, straining to protect Ginny, and keep her out of this litigation, while on the other hand, she had threatened me, and betrayed me to her creepy stepfather, who had been abusing her for years.

God damn that Jane.

"Were there any other women during the course of your marriage to whom you felt attracted to sexually?"

"No."

"What do you think you did, if anything, that led to the breakdown of your marriage?"

I pulled at straws. Judges like to hear that it takes two.

"He didn't like my sarcasm."

"Anything else?"

More straws. No one was going to believe that former judge perfect Nick had a personality disorder, and was clinically insane.

"I probably could have suggested that we go to counseling more emphatically."

"When do you believe your relationship broke down?"

On the honeymoon? "About two years ago."

There followed a long, detailed examination of my bank statements, line by line; of my credit card statements, and my personal expenses. The furniture I bought for the house in Southport. Every dime that I'd spent on Joy, including her insurance, vet, dentist, and farrier, and her show expenses. When all was said and done, the picture was pretty clear. I had been basically renting my right to stay in Nick's two houses, as long as I paid my own bills, and managed our life together. No amount of cash ever passed to me from him in twelve years, until the time that I opened my own office with Denise a year ago.

I had been watching Nick intermittently throughout my deposition. He never once looked at me—he stared over toward the corner of the bookcase, his face was a determined blank. I knew what that meant. Every ounce of acting ability he had was tuned into keeping his anger in check. I knew he was furious.

"Ms. Carbury, what do you buy at Williams-Sonoma?"

"Well," I said slowly, "it's a store that sells equipment for cooking, so I buy cooking equipment there."

"How much would you estimate that you have spent at Williams-Sonoma in the past year?"

"No idea. I had to recreate my entire kitchen."

"How many vacations have you gone on since you left the marital home in Warwick?"

"Define 'vacation.'"

"Trips, places you visited. Places where you stayed other than your home in Southport."

"I took a long weekend in June in Vermont, and a week on Nantucket in September."

"How much did those vacations cost?"

"I don't know."

"Would it surprise you to learn that they cost in excess of three thousand dollars?"

Don chuckled. "With or without food, Mike?"

McAfee bristled. "Is that an objection?"

"No, just having a laugh. These people as a couple spent five or six times that in vacations a year, on average, but you go ahead and nickel and dime my client. After all, it's what her husband did to her for twelve years."

My God, that was good for me. I wanted a cigarette, and I didn't even smoke.

McAfee turned bright red. "Objection!"

Don stood up. "You're the one doing the questions, Mike old boy. I think we're done here, Emma. See you at the trial, gentlemen."

I picked up my purse, and blew a kiss at Nick, who scowled ferociously.

"Well that was a hoot," Don exclaimed, as he threw his big brief-case into the trunk of his Mercedes. "You were great. You never let that oaf ruffle you."

I nodded at the compliment, but mentally I was miles away. I was busily adding up the hours that both those lawyers took to go through every bit of financial discovery before the deposition, and the two plus hours that we had just sat there, plus the cost of the transcript once the court reporter was finished typing it. Thousands of dollars. And the trial was still on the horizon.

Later that day I received an email from Don:

> Hi Emma,
>
> I just got notice from the Clerk's Office. Judge Milo has been transferred to another jurisdiction, so the administrative powers that be are rounding up another judge that won't be disqualified from your case. Your trial has been pushed back to November third.
>
> Keep your chin up!
> Best regards, Don

I sat in my car at the beach and screamed with frustration, pounding my open hands on the steering wheel until they were numb. There was nothing I could do. I was looking forward to yet another month of extreme stress, and time wasted on preparing for trial.

I vowed to never accept another family litigation case again. The experience was just too horrible.

CHAPTER 23

Soul Retrieval

"Shamanic healers are doctors for the soul," Afton explained at our next session. "The word 'shaman' comes from the Tungus tribe in Siberia, and means 'one who sees in the dark.' When a person experiences some kind of trauma, the result is 'soul loss,' meaning that essential parts of our energy have left us. The soul literally escapes the ordeal, in order to survive. Psychotherapists call it 'dissociation.' The trauma may come in the form of violence, physical or sexual, or perhaps a death, or a divorce, or even an operation. Sometimes a portion of the soul, or life energy, is actually stolen by another person, known as a 'psychic vampire'. This occurs when an individual gives up her or his personal power to another. Children, who are completely dependant on adults, are particularly vulnerable."

"I remember once telling Nick that he was sucking the soul out of me, not having a clue about what I was saying at the time."

Afton nodded. "Destructive relationships are particularly harmful, because they are ongoing, and usually involve a betrayal of some kind. They can create *so* much sickness. Shamanic healing is based on the concept that the major causes of physical and mental illness are soul loss. Problems manifest because in fact, no one is at home. These people are not whole. It is important to remember that soul loss will beget more soul loss. That is to say, abusive people have always been abused by someone else. It is a cycle of bad karma that must be stopped, and healed.

"The process of 'soul retrieval' will bring the lost bits of soul, or life essence, back home to the body. The shaman will journey into the nonordinary worlds through an altered state which Michael Harner calls Shamanic State of Consciousness, or SSC. This is accomplished through the monotonous rhythm of percussion instruments, usually the drum." Afton grinned. "So, if you've ever watched an old Western, and the Indians were having a ceremony which involved drumming, you've got an idea of how this works. The scientific theory is that the regular beats produce an elevated number of theta waves in the brain. Many Native American tribes claim that the sounds align their bodies with the pulse of the earth.

"Journeys vary depending on the client. I never know where I will be sent on his or her behalf—to the Lower, Middle, or Upper Worlds. There are many levels in each, but I trust that my guides and power animals will give me the assistance that I need, and keep me safe.

"I tend to combine shamanic journeying and soul retrieval," Afton explained. "It seems to work for my clients. Put simply, my soul leaves my body to take this journey. When I have gathered your lost soul parts, I will blow them back into your body.

"We have to be clear on our intent. What would you like to work on today?"

"I want to feel that my life is moving forward. I feel impatient and trapped at times, and I have trouble sleeping."

Afton thought for a moment. "So you need to feel peace, so that you're in the flow, and not pushing. I know that you're an ambitious woman, but you are actually blocking yourself. A watched kettle never boils."

Afton had me take off my watch and jewelry, and stand like a totem pole, with my arms extended. Using feathers she cleared the energy around me, back and front, over my head, and under both of my feet. She was chanting softly, what she called "opening the space", addressing the four directions, calling her helping spirits to her.

Then she had me lie on the floor, with a bolster under my knees, and a blanket over me. Afton lay down next to me. She started the drumming CD.

"Just breathe normally. I may go to the Lower World, or the Upper World. First, I have to find your power animal. Stay in your body, be present, and let the drum feed you."

I kept my mind clear, and focused on my breathing. I kept wiggling my fingers and toes, assuring myself that I was still in the room.

After about twenty minutes, the drum became louder, and the beat was a succession of rapid thuds, then slower, and then it stopped.

Afton got up, stooped, and blew first, into my heart center, and then into the top of my head. She shook her rattle over me, to seal my retrieved soul parts back into my body.

"Just relax," she whispered. "I need to take some notes."

"Your power animal is a ram," Afton reported, after a few minutes.

"Oh!" I said, surprised. I was expecting her to tell me that it was a hawk, or some other large bird. "I'm an Aries."

"Think about ram energy," she replied. "They are nimble, sure footed, and powerful. They have the innate ability to climb to great heights without fear, and they can be fierce warriors."

"They lock horns," I added. "My dad was also an Aries. I remember my sister using the visual of two rams fighting, to describe our relationship."

"It's interesting that you thought of that," Afton remarked. "Because this journey was all about your father."

I looked at her in horror. "You can't be serious! I spent all of last year clearing my past, especially him." I raised my voice. "Why am I being dragged back there? Enough already!"

Afton was silent for a few moments. I got up, put my jewelry back on, grabbed my coat, and frankly thought about bolting. I felt that I had done everything that I was meant to do—it had required tremendous courage for me to leave my marriage, and then to start my own law firm in the midst of a contested divorce. But I had taken huge leaps of faith, and I was in my current position because of hard work and pure will power. Why was the Universe kicking me in the face—again?

"I don't know what to tell you, Emma. This is what came up. Your lost soul part was your ability to love. I was barely able to coax that bit of you out of the cave where it was hiding. You were about eight. Your head was bald and misshapen, like a baby's, and your eyes were huge and hollow."

"Oh my God!" I cried, and sat down again. "All that work I did with Reiki, and Aromatherapy, and now you're telling me that a huge, fundamental part of me was still missing? Why the hell did I bother?" I was shouting now. This was not Afton's fault, and I didn't care. I felt like I had been duped all over again, just like I had been with Ginny. Was it ever going to end?

"All I can say is that nothing is as powerful as Shamanic healing. It goes deeper than any other form of energy work, and I have tried them all. There are layers to everything. Perhaps you're ready now to address the really tough issues." She paused. "If something from your past still has an emotional charge, then there remains work to be done. I asked your power animal why you were so unwilling to come out of the cave. He said: She's just woken up from a nightmare, and she doesn't want to go back."

I felt bitter. "And yet here you are, hauling me there."

"The point is, you *did* come back. That was the retrieved soul part that I blew back into your body. We had to talk to your dad first."

"WHAT?"

"I asked your permission, and then left you with your ram, while I went to see him. You really like your ram, by the way. You kept hugging him, sticking your face into his wooly shoulder. You said that you loved the way he smelled."

I smiled suddenly. I do the exact same thing with Joy and Abby.

"Your power animal is always there, you know Emma," she said gently. "And he'll never betray you."

What a novel concept. "OK, what did my dad say? I'm ready to hear it." But I wrapped my arms around myself tightly, in anticipation of more pain. I felt suddenly that I could really use a vacation from my life.

"He said that he was really happy that I had come; that he had been wanting to clear this karma with you. He explained that he had been in a terrible place when you were little—lots of self loathing. He didn't know how to love you. The fact that you so obviously loved him was terrifying. He was worried that you would eventually see through him, and then the light would go out of your eyes. So he pushed you away first."

"Oh come on!" I scoffed. "This is psych 101! I was a kid. It was his job to protect me. Instead, he made my life so intolerable, I had to split off and go live in an emotional cave to survive my childhood. How come he was always wonderful to my sister? How about all the incestuous comments he made to me, when I started to develop? Did he explain that?"

"No. But I did bring you in to see him. He apologized to you. He said that he loved you. You put your little hand on top of his open palm."

"So that's it? All better now? Am I done?" I started to gather my things. I took out my check book.

"He said something about the military. Was he in a war?"

"The Korean War. I think he was on a battleship."

"He was suffering from post traumatic stress disorder, Emma."

Soul loss begets soul loss. It explained Dad's obsessions with *M*A*S*H,* and *Top Gun.* Audrey had bought him the DVD's, and he had watched them over and over, for hours at a time.

I took a deep breath. "Look, I hear what you're saying, but what I'm getting is excuses. It was just about him, right?" Ginny all over again. "No god damn thought at all regarding my feelings."

"People who are on vibrations that low can't think of others. All they know how to do is survive."

"I always think of others," I said coldly. Afton seemed full of compassion for my dear departed daddy, and completely oblivious to what I was going through.

Afton tried one more time. "Remember that your soul part is home now, Emma. We talked about this. It means that all the feelings that you escaped so long ago are back too. You'll be integrating that piece of you for a few days. Don't rush it—be gentle with yourself. My guides said to tell you to wear green stones, and eat green vegetables. Do things you used to love when you were a child. Take plenty of salt baths."

"Great. Thanks."

"I know that you're having a difficult time with this, Emma. Sometimes it's just best to surrender to the Universe."

It was then that I truly lost my temper. "SURRENDER! MY ASS! That's the word that armies use in war, when the loser's only options are to die horribly, or wave the white flag. I NEVER

SURRENDER, DO YOU HEAR ME? Not to the Universe, not to my husband, and certainly not ever to my darling daddy, as he was kicking down my bedroom door, and slamming me up against the wall, trying to prove how big and powerful he was. WHOSE SIDE ARE YOU ON?"

I dropped the check on her table, and left.

For about three days I stormed. I could barely speak to anyone, and when I did, it was short, and crisp. Occasionally I felt as though I wanted to cry, but then nothing would come. I just didn't want to waste any more energy on my family, and especially on my father, who had betrayed me on so many levels, I could barely think about it without screaming with rage. His treatment of me had created the pattern of destructive and abusive relationships in my life—a pattern that was still a source of pain and confusion for me. At least I had the pleasure of knowing that this particular journey had ended. Game over.

I knew not to ride Joy when I was feeling so rebellious, so I either long lined her, or let her run around the ring on her own. Watching her buck with delight gave me a sense of freedom. Joy was a goddess, and her extraordinary physical power was a continual source of solace to me. I remembered my friend the ram, as rider free, Joy jumped the course that was set up in the ring. She flew across oxers, turned on a dime, and rolled back with ease.

I would never give my power away again.

CHAPTER 24

Trial

I woke on the morning of my divorce trial, and for a moment, I had no recollection of the day's program. Then in a flash, it came. At least this time the ordeal would be done. No more testifying at hearings and depositions. I would finally be through with Nick Bennington.

Denise met me on the third floor of Ludlow Superior Court. We sat on a bench near the window, and waited for Don. We watched the parade of emotionally distraught people drift by us. Most of the faces were frozen by exhaustion. A few were infused with rage. I surrounded myself with white light, determined to protect myself from the toxicity of the environment. The divorce process was truly insane.

"How do you feel?" Denise whispered.

"A little sick, frankly, but I keep focusing on the promised land to come."

"It may take months for the judge to render a decision, you know," Denise reminded me.

"No matter. With any luck, I will never have to set foot in this horrid building again."

Nick stepped off the elevator, glanced at us briefly, and instantly located a group of good ole boys schmoozing by the Marshal's station. I realized with a shudder that I had lived with the man for over twelve years; sharing meals, vacations, holidays, and assorted family crises. But now he was a complete stranger. In the year that we'd been separated, I had so disconnected from the marriage that Nick was now merely the person who was going to release my money to me when the trial was over. I knew then that I could be detached on the witness stand, because I *was* detached. I felt nothing but compassion for what was left of his life. He had only himself to blame.

Don got off the elevator and came toward us, rolling his heavy file boxes behind him. Once again I saw the airport analogy. This experience was the layover, time served before I was permitted to get on with my life.

"We're all set, Em," Don said, sitting on the bench next to Denise. "Testimony is going to begin promptly at ten in courtroom five. I'll put you on the stand—you know the drill. Just remember that when McAfee gets up for cross, you're the client, not opposing counsel. We want the judge to like you."

I resisted the urge to hit Donald in the head with my purse. I couldn't care less if the judge liked me, hated me, or was just plain bored by me. I knew what I was entitled to from my marriage, and my ability to act like a sweet Warwick homemaker was immaterial. The judge was being paid by the taxpayers to be fair, just, and reasonable in every case before him. Unfortunately, the Connecticut Judicial Department felt differently. Divorce trials in our great state had become popularity contests.

"Did you see their witness list?" Don asked, passing it over. "Nick's bringing in his daughter, Deborah, to testify."

I laughed. "Another scare tactic! He never stops trying, I'll give him that. He'll take a shot at anything to get me to lose it in the courtroom."

"What could this woman say about you?" Don asked.

"Nothing. I was always pleasant and generous. We never even had a disagreement." I thought for a second. "She *may* be coming to describe how sarcastic and impatient I could be with her father."

"Hell," Don grunted. "So was I—on the record. The man is insufferable, and a terrible liar. I'll make short work of her, don't worry."

The judge's clerk was setting up when we entered the courtroom. I followed Don to the counsel table on the right, while Denise took a seat behind the bar. Nick and McAfee sauntered in. There was no sign of Deborah. Just as I thought: Nick used her name to get a rise out of me. He was going to be disappointed.

"How are you all today?" The clerk asked. She was very young, and I remembered how heady it had felt to be just out of law school, and suddenly thrust into the seemingly powerful world of judges and courtroom procedure. Every day, lawyers would charm me, as I was the direct line to my judge, and it had made me a little full of myself. Nearly twenty years later, I knew better. Once I had left the court system, and was looking for a job, my so-called legal buddies had all disappeared.

"Fine, how are you?" Denise returned, too politely.

"Very well, thank you," the young woman said, brightly.

Denise laughed. "We're both good liars, aren't we?"

The clerk's face froze, and she snarled, "I am *not* a liar, counselor, and I'll thank you to remember it!"

Ah yes. Definitely a tad full of herself. But she would learn.

After a few minutes, the court reporter arrived, and the State Marshal had us All rise! as the Honorable Seamus O'Neil entered the courtroom and seated himself at the bench.

"Are the parties ready on *Carbury v. Bennington?*" The judge inquired.

There was a chorus of yes, your honors, the judge ascertained that he had current financial affidavits from both sides, and Donald was instructed to call his first witness.

As I walked up to the witness stand, the right heel of my favorite black pumps caught on the carpet and came off. Maintaining as much dignity as I could, I hobbled up the steps, and was sworn in by Clerk Congeniality.

Don took me through the standard preliminary questions, regarding my educational background, my work experience, and my age and health. Don then began asking questions about the date and location of the marriage, and whether I had been a resident of the State of Connecticut for more than one year, prior to the bringing of the dissolution action.

He made a point of bringing out the fact that I had been a court clerk myself upon graduating from law school, and I was asked to list the judges for whom I had worked. Three of them were currently sitting on the Appellate Bench, and two more were Connecticut Supreme Court Justices. Don was clearly making it difficult for the judge to form a bias toward Nick as being 'one of our own.' I had once been part of the team as well. I had clerked for Nick.

Then Don moved into the financial situation.

"From the time that you were married until today, or until you moved out of the marital home, were there ever any joint accounts with you and Mr. Bennington?"

"Yes."

"What were they?'

"We had a joint Visa account around the time of our marriage, and a joint ExxonMobil card, which I sent back to Nick after I moved out."

"No bank accounts, security accounts, money markets, or anything like that?"

"No."

"When was the joint Visa terminated?"

"About a year after our marriage."

"Under what circumstances did that account close?"

"Nick told me that the new cards were coming in, and that he needed the old one." I paused. "But then he never gave me the new card."

"Did you ever ask him for it?"

"No."

"Why not?"

I sighed. "I don't know." I saw the judge glance over at me, and then at Nick.

"All right. Who did the grocery shopping?"

"I did."

"And how would you pay for that?"

"Nick would write out a check to the Warwick Market, and I would go."

"And you would fill in the amount?"

"Yes."

"Why didn't you write checks from your own account to buy food?"

"My salary, after taxes, barely covers my expenses."

"Before, or after you moved out?"

"Both. It's easier with the temporary alimony, as I am writing the checks myself, but now I have the added expenses of rent, renter's insurance, the credit card bills for my new furniture, utilities. Garbage pick up. Mowing. Leaf and snow removal."

Don smiled. "So less stress, but the numbers haven't changed much?"

"Except for a recent lowering of my horse's board fee, that is correct."

"While you were still living with your husband—having the credit card taken away, being forced to ask for money to buy food, how did that make you feel?"

"Oh, humiliated, devalued, as though I was a child. It was not a good feeling."

Don asked questions about my new practice with Denise, what kind of cases we were taking, and cash flow for the previous year.

He asked about the Connecticut Affiliation of Professional Women.

"What was the reason that you founded this group?"

"It was an idea that I had—I wanted to offer information to women who feel trapped and vulnerable." There was a loud noise from Nick's table. Both men were laughing. I ignored them.

"What is the goal of this Affiliation?"

"There are about fifteen of us in various professions. We are committed to supporting women through divorce and other major life transitions."

"How does the group work?"

"We have meetings every month or so. We have a website, and a publicist."

"What was the idea of having all the different professions in the group?"

"I feel that lawyers just can't cover all the bases. Women need CPAs, financial planners, mortgage and insurance specialists, et cetera."

"So do you network? Do you cross pollinate your cases with each other?"

"Yes. That was the whole point, so that our clients feel a unified system of support behind them."

"What professions are represented, besides the ones that you've mentioned?"

McAfee jumped up. "Objection. Is there any relevance to this?"

Don rolled his eyes. "Attorney McAfee's tone notwithstanding, I think this evidence goes to show the efforts that my client has made in order to generate income."

The judge said: "I'll allow it. For what it's worth."

Another good ole boy. I answered the question quickly, and Donald moved on.

"With respect to the Warwick home, who has title to that home presently?"

"Nick."

"Did he own the property prior to your marriage?"

"Yes."

"What were your responsibilities with respect to that home?"

"I did all of the laundry, all of the food shopping. I cleaned the half of the house that the cleaning lady didn't do."

"Why did the cleaning lady clean only half of the house?"

"Nick wouldn't pay her to do the whole house."

"Did you do anything to make improvements or repairs to the property?"

"I painted walls, trim, and windows. I painted the screen porch and the breezeway every other year. I did most of the landscaping."

"Were there ever any landscapers hired to work on the Warwick property?"

"No."

"What did you do by way of landscaping?"

"Nick had built a couple of fieldstone retaining walls; one in front, one in the back. I turned them into perennial borders. I set up a rock garden on the patio. I started a rose garden, an ornamental bush garden, and an herb garden. I also did all of the work keeping the driveway weeded and cleared—the top by the road is Belgian block, and the remainder, which is very long, is gravel. I painted the front gate, raked leaves, shoveled snow, put down mulch, kept several compost piles going for gardening."

"Why did you do these things?"

I thought for a moment. "I like to keep things beautiful. Home matters to me."

"Did your husband know this?"

"Yes."

"Did he ever hire anyone to do any of this work, so you wouldn't have to?"

"No."

Don walked up to the witness stand. "Can you identify this document?"

"Yes."

"What is it?"

"This is the gardening journal that I kept for the Warwick home, from the time of our engagement, until I left Warwick last year."

"I'd like to offer this as an exhibit, your honor."

McAfee again. "Objection your honor. I have no idea what relevance a gardening journal has. In this case, we have notations in a book. We have some pictures in here. The witness has testified that she liked to garden and did garden. I think this is cumulative, and unnecessary."

Don responded. "I think that this journal is the best evidence of what my client did with respect to the property."

McAfee snarled. "The best evidence is her own direct testimony as to what she did. This offering is irrelevant and unnecessary corroborative evidence."

The judge was clearly bored. "Objection sustained. Move on, Mr. Hall."

I glanced over at Denise, who looked disgusted. She and I both knew that the photographs in my journal were the best evidence of the landscaping work that I had done; work that would have cost thousands of dollars, had it been performed by a professional.

Connecticut divorce law was stuck somewhere around 1950: if it didn't generate income, the activity had no value.

Don rallied. "Ms. Carbury, when you left the Warwick home last fall, did you take with you any furniture, or furnishings?"

"I took three pieces of furniture."

"What were they?"

"I took the chaise from my study. I took my Vanderbilt University chair from the family room. I took a bookcase from one of the guest rooms."

"What else, if anything, did you take?"

"My clothes, my painting supplies, and my books."

"Did you take anything from the kitchen?"

Aha. The great Williams-Sonoma debate. "Just a couple of pots, and my mixer."

"When you moved into your rental home, did you have to furnish it?"

"Yes."

"Where did you go to furnish it?"

"Ethan Allen in Norwalk."

"Did you discuss the furniture situation with your husband before hand?"

"Yes."

"What, if anything, was your understanding, following that discussion?"

"We agreed that I would leave the Warwick house basically status quo, and I would buy new things."

"Now there's also a New Hampshire property that is in Mr. Bennington's name, is there not?"

"Yes."

"And that was owned by him at the time that the two of you were married?"

"Yes."

"Would you please describe that property?"

"It's a three story house, approximately thirty-five hundred square feet of living area, which is located on the water at Pequot Lake. There is a wrap around deck, and a small deck off the master bedroom. There is a fireplace on each level, a large kitchen, three full baths and five bedrooms, plus a dining room, and a living room with a cathedral ceiling."

"How often would you and Mr. Bennington go up to New Hampshire to use that property?"

"It was very regular. Weekends, holidays, and summers."

"How often in a month's time?"

I grinned. "If Dartmouth was playing a home game, either football, or hockey, we were there."

"Did you entertain up there?"

"Often."

"How often?"

"Whenever Dartmouth was home, we had at least one Dartmouth couple staying with us. Sometimes two or three. This was also true of Reunions."

"What if anything did you have to do with respect to those weekends?'

"I did all the cleaning, all of the laundry, all the bedroom set up, all the food shopping, and most of the cooking, if we stayed in for meals."

"Was there ever help employed with respect to the lake property?"

"Not until about two years before I moved out. I finally got Nick to agree to hire a cleaning person."

"How often did that cleaning person come?"

"When I knew that we would be up there, I would call and arrange with her to come in."

"Okay. Other than going to New Hampshire, did you and Mr. Bennington take any vacations?"

"Yes."

"Where did you go?"

"Nick's friends from Dartmouth like to take trips together. We went to San Francisco, Vail, New Orleans, and Chicago. I also went with him to three or four hockey tournaments in Canada; specifically—Vancouver Island, Ottawa, Montreal and Quebec City. I attended several Navy events as well, usually in Newport, or Maine."

"We also took various trips overseas," I continued. "We went to London and Western England, Scotland, ten days in Paris, and Provence. We took a cruise that was also a Dartmouth trip. The cruise began in the North of France—Normandy and Brittany. The ship went on to various places in the British Isles, including Cornwall, two stops in Ireland, the Inner Hebrides, and the Orkney Islands. The trip ended in Edinburgh."

"Is it fair to say that the two of you did a lot of travelling in your marriage?'

"Yes."

"Ms. Carbury, do you feel that your marriage has broken down irretrievably?"

"Yes."

"Why do you feel that your marriage has broken down?"

"The two main reasons were Nick's control of the money, and the fact that our sex life was unsatisfying to me."

"Regarding your sex life, did you ever try to discuss that with your husband?"

"Many times."

"And did you ever make any suggestions of therapy or anything like that?"

"Yes."

"And what was his response?"

"He didn't want to talk about it."

"Have you had sexual relations with any other persons since the date of your marriage?"

"No."

"Did you in any way contribute to the breakdown of your marriage?"

Play the game. "Oh, I'm sure that I did. It takes two."

"In what ways do you think that you contributed to the breakdown of your marriage?"

"I can be very sarcastic, and I know that he didn't like that. I can be impatient."

"Ms. Carbury, with respect to your claims for relief, and proposed orders for the court, you are asking for a lump sum asset division, first and foremost, is that correct?"

"Correct."

"What is the reason that you want a lump sum, rather than periodic alimony?"

I took a deep breath. "Because I want to be done with the control, and I'm afraid that if I am awarded periodic alimony, we will be back in here with motions to modify, and more control. I've had enough."

"OK. Now, there are items that you would like to retrieve from the New Hampshire property, is that correct?"

"Yes."

"What are those items?"

"Some clothing, books, my painting supplies, and various items of sporting equipment."

"You would like to be given access to go get this personal property, is that correct?"

"Yes."

Don looked up at the judge. "Your honor, I don't know if you would like to take the mid-morning break at this time? I just need a quick run-through of my notes to see if I have anything left."

The judge nodded. "Fine. Let's do that. We'll take a fifteen minute recess."

The clerk came back into the courtroom almost immediately, and Don and McAfee followed her to have a discussion with the judge in chambers.

"You were great Em!" Denise reported enthusiastically. "Your testimony was razor sharp. No emotion, except at the very end, and you didn't rip into Nick. Judges are always looking out for that."

"I know. That's the problem with this fucking system," I said, angrily. "Awards are based on acting ability. Only, I wasn't acting. I'm so dead tired of Nick, this case, and our so-called marriage, I just want to finish today, and get the hell out of here. I don't want to waste another moment of my life on the man."

Don came out. He was smiling. "Ladies, the judge is furious with the other side. 'Why are we here, counselors?' were the first words out of his mouth. He's sending us down the hall to Judge Pinkus—to see if we can settle."

I frowned. "Hal Pinkus? He's a hockey buddy of Nick's. I don't like the sound of this."

Don picked up his briefcase. "It's all we've got, Em. Every judge in this building has worked or socialized with Nick in the past. O'Neil is the only one who hasn't had the pleasure. Either we play along, or we postpone the trial until we can find someone else to pre-try this file."

Denise and I looked at each other in dismay. My feet were in the fire—what could I do?

"Fine. But I don't want to hear that you all sat around in chambers scratching your testicles for two hours, while I get the shaft."

"Language, Attorney Carbury!" Don chuckled. "Duly noted. I promise to be the only woman in the room."

An hour later, Don came back with a convoluted offer, ostensibly from McAfee. "It's clear that Nick is running this show," Don grunted. "And Mike is just the puppet. More control games. Nick really doesn't want to let you out of his clutches, Emma." He shook his head with disbelief. "He's a nightmare!"

"Yes," I replied, with feeling. "Are you recommending this travesty of a settlement?"

"Oh no, just reporting. Round two is about to begin."

At one o'clock the entire courthouse shut down for lunch. Don, Denise and I walked around the corner to the diner, and ordered. Just as the waiter had moved away, we watched with a mixture of disgust and amusement as Judge O'Neil and Judge Aimée Colger-Smyth strolled in, and were seated.

"Pretty obvious that she's looking for an update," Denise said through her teeth. "Could that woman be any more stupid?"

"I don't see how," Don replied. "She should have done her pumping in private. Now there's a definite appearance of impropriety in this case. She'd better hope that we settle today."

"I wonder how much 'pumping' she and Nick did in the past," I said, trying to laugh. "I guess we'll never know now."

Finally, just before four o'clock, Nick came up with a settlement offer that I could live with.

"Seven-fifty, Emma," Don announced, "which if you recall, was my original estimate. Five hundred thousand within the next thirty days, and the remaining two-fifty on or before a year from today's date. Each of you pays your own debts, attorney's fees, et cetera."

"It's a deal," I said, with obvious relief. Denise hugged me, and hurried back to the office to put out some fires. Don and I proceeded up to the law library, to draft the agreement. He used his laptop for the boiler plate language, and then emailed the document to himself on the court computer, to print it out.

As I was plaintiff, I was to testify at the uncontested hearing. Judge Pinkus heard us. Don thought it was better to leave O'Neill open, in case we had problems in the future.

"We won't," I said. "I know my husband. Nick has lost the battle, so he's done with me. He'll be looking for new prey now."

And so, we were divorced. The judge found our agreement to be fair and equitable, and he entered a decree of uncontested dissolution of marriage based on irretrievable breakdown. I walked down from the stand, kissed Don on the cheek right in front of my now ex-husband, and sashayed out the door.

Downstairs in the lobby, I started skipping, hoping that the duct tape on my shoe would hold. The Marshals at the metal detector laughed as I executed a couple of twirls, before heading out the revolving door.

I was a free woman.

Chapter 25

Freedom

Exactly one week after my divorce, Annie came in to my office, and shut the door quietly. She leaned over my desk. "Emma, there's a Virginia Sherman here to see you."

I froze. Ginny.

I got up without saying a word, and Annie followed me out to the waiting area. Ginny was sitting in a chair in the farthest corner. She was dressed in brown riding breeches, and a brown suede jacket, and her hair was pulled back from her thin face in one long braid. She looked like a teenager, and she had dropped about thirty pounds.

"Hey," she said, standing up. "I hope this is OK."

I said that it was, but I didn't move any nearer. Annie asked if she'd like something to drink.

"I'm fine, thanks." Ginny looked at me. "Can we talk?"

I had a flash of us sitting in my office, surrounded by law books and files, and all of my certificates on the walls. I didn't want her to feel like she had been sent to the principal's office.

I grabbed my coat. "Let's take a walk along the river."

The waves of her misery were palpable, as always. It occurred to me that this was the first time I had ever seen Ginny outside of the horse world. Then I realized: her power over me was gone. The connection was broken. I really was free.

But I still felt compassion. Huge, shiny pink bubbles of compassion. Was that the definition of unconditional love? Ginny had caused me *so* much confusion and pain. Lisa and I were no longer speaking, tack shop employees were snubbing me, and Ginny had indirectly made my divorce even more difficult. But I still wanted to help her.

We circled the building, and headed south on the path by the water. There was a bench near some boat slips, and Ginny sat down. Curious, I followed suit.

"Why have you come here Ginny?"

Her face was gaunt; her cheek bones stuck out, her chin was a sharp point, and her eyes had dark circles under them. "I can't sleep." She replied. "Too much turning over in my head, I guess."

I looked at her with concern. "Flashbacks?"

She seemed surprised. "How did you know?"

"Research. Severe trauma is almost always accompanied by flashbacks."

Ginny sighed. "I should have read those books that you mention in your article." She seemed to rally a little. "Look Emma, I'm so sorry. I screwed up. I told my…stepfather about you, and he flipped. I was trying to score off him, and off you, and it backfired. He dictated that letter, and I typed it. I'm not going to tell you that I fought real hard, either. That would be a lie," she frowned, "and I'm done with lying. It got worse at home after that. The control. It was like being in prison. One day I couldn't stand it any more, and I went to see your friend, the psychologist. Randy? We've been working together now for a few months. She has a group—I go on Tuesday nights. Did she tell you?"

This was a pleasant surprise. "No! But I'm so glad! Are these sessions helping?"

"I think so. We're working on getting me to the point where I feel safe enough to move off my parents' estate. Randy sent me to a lawyer. She's in your Affiliation, the one who does trusts."

"Nan?"

"Yeah. She's dealing with my trust fund. She says we can cut some kind of deal, so that I get my money, and I can live my own life. Nan's pretty sure that my family isn't going to make a big fuss."

"Because of the publicity if you go to court? She's right about that."

"Good! I wanted to know what your reaction was, before I said yes to anything. It all seems clear when they talk, but most of the time, I'm just so scared."

"What scares you the most Ginny?"

She swallowed. Her neck was so thin, it was really pronounced.

"I'm afraid that I can't manage on my own, that I can't take care of things—myself. That I'll do something stupid, or forget something, and everyone will see right through me. They'll know that I'm different. I couldn't bear that."

I was silent for a bit. I knew that the worst thing for me to do would be to tell her that her feelings were wrong. But what I wanted to say was that everyone feels like that, at least part of the time.

"I think that it has everything to do with confidence, in yourself, and in the people with whom you've placed your trust. When and if you do experience shakiness, knowing that there's someone you can count on to help, that's the key. The best case scenario is a friend, of course, but if it's someone that you pay to help you, that's good too."

Ginny focused down river. We watched a fisherman cast his line off a dock. "I don't know how to make friends, Emma. I never could. How could I talk about boys, and make-up, and going to parties? With all the craziness going on in my house? All I know about is horses."

"Well for starters, don't send your friends certified nasty-grams if they get too close!"

She grinned. "No huh? That didn't work for you?"

"It most definitely did not."

"Does that mean that we're still friends?"

I turned so that I was facing her. To Ginny's credit, she didn't flinch. I know how intimidating I can be, especially in a suit, but of course she was used to intimidation.

"Here's the deal, Virginia. We can be friends under the following conditions, known in the psychotherapy world as 'boundaries.' First, no more head games at night. You have something to say to me, call me, text me, send me a carrier pigeon. And not a threatening carrier pigeon, damn it!"

She grinned again.

"Second, I do not respond to manipulative, dramatic control tactics. In fact, I won't put up with drama of any description. Just ask my ex husband."

"You nailed him to the wall in your divorce?"

"I sure as hell did."

"Good for you. OK, no bullshit. Got it. Third?"

"Third," I took several deep breaths. "What was with the lesbian thing? All power to those ladies, but I'm not one of them, and never was. I haven't had a man come on to me as, er, creatively as you did. What was going on there?"

Her thin face clouded over. "Time for another apology. I just wanted to see how you'd react. It was a game, like you said. I liked you, and I liked how you love your horse, so I kinda wanted to punish you for that. I wanted the power to upset you. I think I was a little jealous."

"So you're not attracted to me?"

"I don't know. Maybe. I doubt that I'm attracted to anyone, to be honest. For most of my life I've felt that all I was good for was sex. I've used it to mess with people, mostly men. But there have been women too—classmates in college, girls who ride. Randy says that once I heal, I will see my real self worth, or something. And then I won't need to bait nice folks like you. Sorry." She looked sheepish.

Again I thought of all the trouble she had caused. Did I really want to be friends with this woman?

She knew what I was thinking. "I understand if you don't want anything more to do with me. I seem to dump piles of my garbage wherever I go."

I made a decision. "If you are willing to have a joint session with me at Randy's, to talk about this, then the answer is yes; we can work on a friendship."

"Cool beans! I could do that! Thanks."

We got up, and began our walk back to the office.

"You're welcome. And by the way, you're paying her fee."

I walked into the nail salon in Westport the next day after work, hoping for a manicure and pedicure. An extremely good looking Asian young man escorted me to a chair, and proceeded to give me the best spa pedicure that I had ever had. I felt so relaxed and safe that I started to nod off in the chair, and eventually came back to earth when my leg massage had ended, and he was putting flip flops on my feet. After my manicure, I received a hot towel shoulder rub as my nails dried. I tipped the man more than the usual twenty percent, and resolved to be open to male masseurs from then on.

Something to look forward to.

When I arrived home that evening, there was a thick envelope from the Connecticut Watercolor Society. The painting that I had submitted for this year's show, *West Cove on Pequot Lake*, had been accepted. As this was my second juried exhibition, I was entitled to become a signature member of CWS. This designation afforded me professional status as a watercolor artist. An application for membership was enclosed.

I called my painting teacher to relay the news.

"That's phenomenal Emma!" Pam exclaimed. "They're very picky. You can start signing your paintings CWS after your name, like I do. Are you going to the gallery opening?"

"May I share a ride with you? I hate attending these things alone."

"Absolutely. We'll go on to a celebratory dinner after the reception. I know a great Italian place in Farmington. This is a very big deal, Emma, and I couldn't be more proud of you!"

"Thanks Pam, but my success has everything to do with your teaching. When I started working with you six years ago, I didn't know one end of a paint brush from another. I had never even heard of neutral tint!"

"You have talent, Emma," Pam said, a serious note in her voice. "Please continue with your art. It's lucky that you started painting at such an early age; you have years to develop your style, and get your work out there. Considering what you have just been through, the timing of this achievement is especially impressive. Well done."

Abby and I drove up to the New Hampshire house the next day to retrieve my personal items. There had already been a snow fall. The lake water looked black against the white of the beach, and the birches were especially stark, with the dark green of the pine trees behind them. I packed up my belongings, loaded them in to my car, and stood with Abby on the deck, facing Pequot Lake. This was goodbye. I had been coming to this house for nearly fourteen years.

"What do you think, Abby?" I picked her up, and hugged her furry little body to me. "Do you think that we'll be even happier at our own lake some day?"

We watched a beaver swim across to the island. His body created a V shaped wake that spread wider and wider as he moved. The loons had already left for the winter, but plenty of song birds were still fluttering about in the bare branches.

"Shall we send a message to Macduff?" I asked Abby.

Abby gave out one loud bark. It rang in my ears, and reverberated against the trees in the stillness. A moment later, we heard another bark echo back.

We had our first snowfall on the coast the following week; about five inches. The day after Thanksgiving, Angela and I met at Sherwood Island State Park in Westport with our cross country skis. It was an odd contrast, skiing on the beach, as the waves rolled in. We could see the fuzzy outline of Long Island, across the Sound.

"How was Thanksgiving at your sister's?" Angela asked, struggling to ski up a snow drift. "Did your mother behave?"

"She wasn't there!" I replied, puffing a little. "Audrey flew down to Florida to stay with friends and to look at a condo."

"Is she planning to move?"

"Not sure. It might just be a snowbird winter thing, so I'd still have to avoid my family during the holiday season every year."

"Did you and Kate have a chance to talk?"

"Not really. Tom's family was in residence, and there was a lot of activity with all of the kids. My sister seems to thrive on chaos."

"And you don't."

"No. I can't stand to be around it, frankly, and I got out of her house as soon as I could without appearing to be rude. You know what Ange? I don't think I can be close to my sister anymore, and it hurts."

"I'm sure it does. Like I said, she's stuck in your mother's world. She'll have more children, and give up more and more power to her husband, and then resent him for it later on."

"Kate will be living in sacrifice, just as Audrey did. If she follows the same path as our mother, she'll take her dissatisfaction out on her kids. But that's not my problem."

"It's not. You're free now! You have plenty of good friends to sustain you, and a growing practice. You're healthy, you love the outdoors, and you're a really good person. I think that as we evolve, it's inevitable that we lose friends and relatives along the way. Life will improve though. I find that it's the reward for creating space. Better people will come."

I laughed. "Speaking of which! I have a date tomorrow night!"

"Ha! With the hot Judge Melnick?"

"Yes. He stopped me in the hall when I was in court on Monday."

"How romantic. You've been divorced all of five minutes. He must have been watching the file on the Judicial Website. Where are you going?"

"Would you believe to the Warren Inn, on Lake Washington? His suggestion. The Universe keeps pulling me up to Litchfield County."

"So, a long drive, each way. Plenty of time to talk. Lovely dinner overlooking the water. Bedrooms upstairs, if required. What will you call him?" Angela wondered. "Or will you just scream Oh God! through each orgasm?"

I could feel my face turning red. "He has asked me to call him

Andy, for your information, and I'm having trouble remembering what an orgasm that wasn't self induced feels like."

"It will come back," Angela said drily. "But you're definitely a penis girl? No more nonsense about being a lesbian?"

"Nope. All done, thanks!"

Angela smirked. "When this gets out, it will certainly be one in the eye for Nick."

"I thought of that. What did all his nasty energy slurping get him in the end? Abby and I moved out, Mac's gone to the Happy Hunting Ground. Nick's all alone in those two houses, probably furious that he has to do his own laundry and buy his own groceries every week. His kids only call when they need something—usually money. It will never occur to him that he has created his empty hell for himself."

"Again, not your problem."

I sighed with relief. "Not any more, thank goodness!"

We stopped to watch the seagulls swoop over the waves, searching for dinner.

"Have you been to see Afton since your soul retrieval?" Angela asked.

"No," I replied. "But I've spoken to her. I left her place rather abruptly after our session, and I wanted to apologize for my behavior."

"I'm sure she's used to it. This shamanic stuff sounds pretty intense."

"It's intense, and it's weird. You really have to want to heal, because going through all that pain again is no fun."

"But the experience is worth it, right?" Angela looked worried. "I didn't tell you. I made an appointment for next week with Afton. I told her that we were friends from way back."

I thought for a moment. "Listen, Ange. I've been exploring various methods of energy healing because I like fast results, and a few days of feeling crazy sure beats ten years in a shrink's chair, getting pumped full of pills the whole time."

"If that helps at all."

"Exactly."

"So, am I missing something here?"

"It's about what resonates with you, that's all. All the research that I've done says 'take what works for you, and leave the rest.' After my soul retrieval with Afton, I went in for a Reiki session. Marilyn and I talked about it, and I've come to the conclusion that Afton's style of Shamanic doesn't work for me. It's too heavy and dark. Every tribe has different traditions, so I will continue to journey by myself, and perhaps some day I'll meet the right practitioner. Randy says that there are plenty of shamanic healers out there who work with a much lighter energy, from a place of love rather than pain."

"Oh. Maybe I should cancel my appointment."

"That's entirely up to you. My best advice is to go with your gut. If I've learned anything from this experience, it's that in the end we have to tune out all the noise around us, and make our own decisions. I'm pulling back for a while simply because my control button is getting pushed—again. I keep hearing about the concept of free will, but in my opinion, it's all bunk. We—all of us here on this planet—are being yanked on constantly. By our so-called guides, by past trauma, by whatever role play we agreed to before we arrived here. Either we do what the Universe wants, or we suffer for not listening. There isn't a blessed moment in a day when I feel that I'm actually making an independent choice about anything. We're all being driven like cattle. It's obnoxious."

"Look Em," Angela said slowly. "You just finished a pretty awful divorce. Even without kids, Nick really put you through it. Add the Ginny/Jane drama to the mix, the move, the new office, two new barns in a year—that's a lot for one person who has virtually no family support. My guess is, and please don't hate me! My guess is that there is still plenty of work for you to do. Speaking from personal experience—divorce takes a big chunk out of you, and I didn't even go to trial. Give yourself a break. No one is judging you."

"No?"

"No," Angela said firmly. "That's all left over gunk from your family. Clear it all out as fast you can, retrieve whatever bits of you are still floating around out there, and try to relax. You'll get the life that you want."

"Promise? Because I really am *so* bored with talking about my past."

"Promise. You deserve it."

"I finally looked up the symbology of seals," I reported, after a few minutes of silent skiing. "They represent active imagination and creativity. Seals are amphibious, so they spend a lot of time in the water, but they are also grounded. Water is symbolic of the feminine, and emotions."

"But that's you all over!" Angela exclaimed. "You've always been open to new adventures, but at the same time, you are the most reliable, level headed person that I know. It's a gift, so I hope that you're grateful."

I thought about this. The last couple of years had been beyond awful, but I'd made enormous changes, and was better for it.

"Grateful. Hmmm. I'm grateful that the nightmare is over—literally. No more psychic vampires! Look what happens if they don't attempt to heal. Nick is a lonely, bitter man. Your ex husband's lawyer has been black listed by every judge in Fairfield County. Vicky and George are dead. Vicky's husband is being charged with murder, as well as fraud. My ex client Marianne is in bankruptcy. Audrey has lost her eldest daughter."

"And your dad is still trying to heal from the Other Side."

I grinned. "That too."

"But what about Ginny? She's your big success story, isn't she? I never thought that someone as damaged as she has been could come around, but she has. Thanks mostly to you."

"Well. Thanks to the women's alliance that Denise and I formed, anyway. Ginny says that feeling that unified support behind her made all the difference to her decision."

"Her stepfather is surely the definition of psychic suck. What do you think will happen to him?"

"In this life? Probably nothing. He'll buy Ginny's silence, and once she does the energy work, she'll be free. She's already warned her brothers and her cousins, all of whom have young daughters. His bloated corporation will continue to sell people drugs that don't help them, and his toxic energy will keep polluting our planet." I paused, and smiled. "For a time anyway. But the Universe will get Douglas in the end, never fear. I believe in karma."

Recommended Reading

Psychic Vampires, Protection from Energy Predators & Parasites,
    by Joe H. Slate, Ph.D., Llewellyn Publications (2002).

Energy Vampires, A Practical Guide for Psychic Self-Protection,
    by Dorothy Harbour, Destiny Books (2002).

Nine Deadly Venoms by Alex Gordon, Ebuilders, Ltd. (2004).

Heaven and Earth by James Van Praagh, Simon & Schuster, Inc. (2001).

The Other Side and Back by Sylvia Browne with Lindsay Harrison,
    Penguin Group (USA) Inc. (1999).

Awakening to the Spirit World by Sandra Ingerman & Hank Wesselman,
    Sounds True Inc. (2010).

Soul Retrieval, Mending the Fragmented Self by Sandra Ingerman,
    HarperCollins (1991).

The Way of the Shaman by Michael Harner, HarperCollins Publishers
    (1990).

Shaman, Healer, Sage by Alberto Villoldo, Ph.D., Harmony Books (2000).

Spirit Healing by Mary Dean Atwood, Sterling Publishing Co., Inc. (2006).

Foundation for Shamanic Studies. . . . . . .www.shamanicstudies.com

Sandra Ingerman . . . . .www.sandraingerman.com

Society of Shamanic Practitioners. . . . . . .www.shamansociety.org

Carla Meeske . . . . .www.spirithealer.com

About the Author

Author Karen A. Stansbury practiced law in Connecticut for twenty-four years. After enduring twenty years of courtroom litigation she became certified in mediation, hoping for a more peaceful life. She began posting helpful articles on her website, encouraging clients to choose a less stressful path to problem solving. Writing novels using real cases was the next logical step. Now she does it full time.

When Karen isn't writing or traveling, she's painting watercolor landscapes, or riding, or kayaking, or biking, or rowing, or cooking, or gardening. She lives in Litchfield County, Connecticut.